Within this Covenant

**Confession and Community
in the Lord's Supper**

Over the years I, like many, have become ever more concerned about the Christian community I live in and my relationships with other believers. I am far from perfect and the struggle to live with others is often agonizing due to my own faults. This manuscript is intended for the sole purpose of study as others join me in thinking about the sacrament of Communion, the Lord's Supper, and what God intended for us as Christians. In no way do I wish to appear dogmatic but rather to be a recipient of God's grace. If you find that you disagree with what I have written, then please spend more time studying God's Word to determine what God intended. May his grace overflow above and beyond to all those who seek him.

All Biblical quotations from the New International Version, Zondervan Bible Publishers, © 1973, 1978, 1984

Within This Covenant published by
Morten Moore Publishing
PO Box 881
Flagstaff, AZ 86002

Copyright 2017
All rights reserved to Ken and Ruth Mortenson
ISBN 978-0-9991108-1-2

1. Religion 2. Christian Practice 3. Sacraments

Printed in the United States and Distributed by Ingram Spark

*To my loving husband,
Ken Mortenson
and
To Darlene J. and Mike B. for your encouragement as
I struggled through those early passages in life.
Thank you for your kind words.*

Over the centuries, the word Communion has become synonymous with the Lord's Supper.

I have used both terms to describe the sacrament of sharing the wine and bread in commemoration of Jesus' death and resurrection.

Contents

In Common: The Bread and The Wine 1

Chapter 1
Breaking the Bread 7

Chapter 2
The Covenant 17

Chapter 3
Committed 37

Chapter 4
A Sacrament of Living Blood 49

Chapter 5
Celebration: Joy 65

Chapter 6
Examining the Uncomfortable 75

Chapter 7
Flesh to the Scaffold 91

Chapter 8
Melting Hearts 99

Chapter 9
As One 109

After Word 117

Within This Covenant

In Common:
The Bread and The Wine

"They devoted themselves to the apostles' teaching and to the fellowship, to the breaking of bread and to prayer. Everyone was filled with awe, and many wonders and miraculous signs were done by the apostles. All the believers were together and had everything in common. Selling their possessions and goods, they gave to anyone as he had need. Every day they continued to meet together in the temple courts. They broke bread in their homes and ate together with glad and sincere hearts, praising God and enjoying the favor of all the people. And the Lord added to their number daily those who were saved." Acts 2:42-47

The First Century

Communion, this sacrament we call the Lord's Supper, began so simply: A loaf of bread, a cup of wine, 12 men united as one. Over the centuries, as the church of Christ has split into various denominations, one element has remained the same. We meet together over bread and wine. Take a moment to consider the definition of the word, Communion.

Com-mun-ion:
   1) the act of sharing; possession in common; participation.
   2) the act of sharing one's thoughts and emotions with another or others, intimate converse.
   3) a group of Christians professing the same faith and practicing the same rites; denomination. 1

For Christians, what began with one man and his followers has multiplied through faith and tradition to become a rich tapestry, practiced in almost every congregation of believers. Regardless of denomination, we practice a tradition of partaking of bread and wine in commemorating Jesus' death and resurrection for us. In the pages that follow we will examine this sacrament in detail. Before we begin, I wish to catch a glimpse of this tradition in some of the denominations spread across North America.

The Twenty-First Century

The Cathedral

An older woman, her fragile body bent by disease, creeps out of the pew. She is followed by a young man, the angular planes of his tanned face at peace, walking down the aisle under the soaring nave of a grand cathedral. One by one, men and women, rise to approach the altar. Each person kneels at a railing in front of the altar, moving one hand across his or her chest, first horizontally and then vertically in the sign of the cross. A priest, clad in a long white robe,
approaches each participant, dipping a small wafer into the wine, then placing the wafer lightly on their tongue. The congregants flow back down the aisle to their individual seats.

The College Campus

Moving on, we visit a home shared by a group of students near any college campus. The shadows of a small candle flicker across the walls as young men and women form a circle around the perimeter of a dim room. A young man picks up a home-made loaf of bread, breaking it in two, before setting the it back on the tray and passing the contents around the circle. Each participant breaks off a small portion, passing the tray around the circle. The other students follow his example, one by one. In turn, a small cup is passed around, each one taking a small sip. As the cup comes around to the leader, he picks up a guitar. Strumming softly, he begins to sing, "We are one in the spirit, we are one
in the Lord."

An American Indian Reservation

We next visit the sun-blasted plains of the Navajo Indian Reservation in the arid southwest. Dusty-skin men pick up the plastic platters and make their way to the front of the church. The leader speaks in choppy, idiomatic syllables, echoing through the sparsely furnished room. Torn linoleum covers the floor under folding chairs set in rows. A fly buzzes loudly across the open space. The eyes of a small boy, leaning into his mother's shoulder, follow the erratic flight of the loud insect.

The usher, dressed in jeans and a faded plaid shirt, passes a plate of fry bread wafers to a woman, narrowly avoided the grimy reach of a little brown hand that strays upward. Both the man and woman smile down at the boy, the usher briefly squeezing his shoulder as he moves to the next row.

"This is my body." The words, spoken in native dialect,

echoes out into the dusky evening.

The Inner City

We move on to a small building set on a grimy street in one of our large cities. The church is squeezed between multi-story buildings lined with the iron ladders of fire escapes. Cardboard covers a broken window as the cost of replacing a single pane of glass has grown beyond the means of the impoverished congregation. The men and women of this little congregation count it a greater blessing as their echoes of vibrant music bounce out onto the trash-strewn streets. Old men in shiny, fraying suits pass the plate from hand to hand with young men, pants sagging from their hips, hair twisted in dreadlocks. As the music rises to a crescendo, a black matron bounces to her feet, her hands in the air. "Thank you, Jesus." Others take up the phrase, their cries reaching the ears of those who hurry past the front doors. As they pass the plate to each other, wide smiles crease joyful faces.

And In the Suburbs

Finally, we approach a church in the suburbs of a large city. The sonorous voice of the leader fills the quiet auditorium.

"If you have accepted Jesus as Lord and Savior of your life, if you have asked his forgiveness for your sins, you are welcome to join us in this Communion."

Again, the plate is passed through the hands of the congregation, row by row, until all had been served. As one, they place the fragments of bread on their tongues, draining tiny plastic cups of juice. As one they stand, singing the final hymn releasing the congregation from the wood-paneled sanctuary.

In Common

Five individual congregations, each with a unique tradition of celebrating communion and yet, we see the common elements in each gathering of believers. Whether you believe that this is the body of Christ becoming one with you or you believe that Communion is more symbolic, the fact remains: Communion calls us to the cross. Whether you live on a wind-strafed reservation or on the asphalt pavement of the inner city, you and I share in a common faith, remembering the resurrection that has changed our lives forever.

When we step aside from our daily routine and contemplate all that is encompassed by Communion, does the act of remembrance come alive? Is our common partaking of bread and wine, the heartbeat of our life within the community? Does Communion end with a starchy wafer?

When he spoke the words, "Do this in remembrance of me," Jesus must have known that the community of believers on earth would debate the meaning of two simple elements necessary to daily life. What did he intend by instituting this sacrament? How does this sacrament become an integral part of our walk with God? Those are the questions we will consider in the following pages. We will first look at how Communion began, then at the meaning of the elements followed by a discussion of how Communion draws us into the community of believers as God intended.

Let us begin by taking a walk along a dark street in Jerusalem in the first century. The stone walls rise overhead, their surface cool to the touch of our fingers. Already the warmth of the day is fading as the sun sets. This is a sacred time. The Jewish celebration of Passover is about to begin. Hurry! We must be indoors before night falls.

Chapter 1

Breaking the Bread

In the fading light, the gray rock walls reflected the evening's fading light into the dark alleys that wound through the ancient city. Two men, returning from the open-air market, climbed the stairway along a limestone wall to the second story of a small home overlooking the narrow alley. Opening the door, a warm glow from oil lamps on a small table spilled out into the street. Then, the darkness closed in as the door was shut against the cool evening air. Within the room, several men reclined on small platforms while others gathered around a basin of water to wash the dust from their faces. Sandals, their straps limp on the cool stone floor, lay discarded near the door.

The two men began arranging the contents of their parcels on the small table, a roasted lamb, wafers of flat bread and a bundle of herbs, their bitter scent spreading across the little room. One of the men set out a large clay bottle of lightly fermented wine. The food was greeted by hungry glances from the others in the room. The group of men had arrived at the two-story dwelling in the late afternoon, after traveling steadily the last few hours to reach their destination before darkness shrouded the city.

Passover, in Jerusalem, the goal of every Jew at least

once in his lifetime. To celebrate Passover in the shadow of the magnificent temple was at the heart of Jewish worship. In the valleys below the city, the white walls of the temple on the hilltop gleaming a welcome to pilgrims as climbing the last few miles of their pilgrimage. They had come to the home of the ancient king, David. This band of men was one of many come to spend Passover in Jerusalem. One of them sent word ahead that they would celebrate the feast of Passover in this small room, the second story of a home built in the shadow of the inner wall that had once protected the homes of Israel's kings.

Passover took the Jews back to a day when they had thrown off the cloak of slavery and emerged free to claim their inheritance, their promised land on the shores of the Mediterranean Sea.

Passover was a time to commemorate the coming of the Angel of Death who passed over the homes of the Jews, which were protected by a smear of blood across the lintel and door posts of each home. Each home procured a roasted lamb as a sign of sacrifice for the blood that covered those inside. They gathered the bitter herbs that recalled their sorrows in Egypt under bondage. Flat bread, made without yeast, graced each table to recall their sudden flight from slavery, their surge into freedom. With each cup of wine, they recalled their heritage and God's provision for the descendants of Abraham, Isaac and Jacob, the patriarchs of the Jewish people.

As the little band of men shared the Passover meal, one took up the bread and extended his hand toward the cup of wine. Then he paused. Looking around he proclaimed, "I tell you the truth, one of you will betray me."

Alarmed, the men began to look at each other. Soon one whispered to another. Who would do this? They had lived together for nearly three years, traveling along dusty roads, sharing meals and going without when there was no food. Why would their leader predict that one of them would turn against him? One by one, they whispered their inquiries.

"Surely not I?"

He waited, watching their confusion. And then Jesus said, "The one who has dipped his hand into the bowl with me will betray me."

Several glanced down at their hands to ensure that they were no where near the common bowl. Others glanced away, hiding their consternation that they had shared a chunk of bread dipped in the wine with their leader.

After a moment, Jesus added, "The Son of Man will go as it has been written about him. But woe to that man who betrays the Son of Man! It would be better for him if he had not been born."

In the moment that followed, one last man leaned toward him.

"Surely not I, Rabbi?" asked Judas.

Jesus glanced at him briefly as he answered, "Yes, it is you."[1]

Did the others understand? From the narrative, it doesn't seem that they did. The group continued eating, taking small sips of wine. Once again, Jesus picked up a loaf and thanked God for the bread as they looked on. Then he broke it in half and passed a piece to either side, around the group, instructing them, "Take and eat; this is my body."

Puzzled they looked at each other before breaking off a piece of the loaf. It was not uncommon for Jesus to say things that were not clear to the rest of them. Without further explanation, he picked up the clay bottle, but did not pour the wine into his cup. This was the fourth cup of wine with the Passover meal, a symbol of hope for the deliverance the Messiah would bring.

Once again, he offered up a prayer of thanksgiving for the wine and passed the cup to the other men, without first taking a sip. "Drink from it, all of you. This is my blood of the covenant, which is poured out for the forgiveness of sins. I tell you, I will not drink of this fruit of the vine from now on, until that day when I drink it anew with you in my Father's kingdom." 2

This little band of men had been with Jesus one hot afternoon as he taught a large crowd that had crowded into every inch of space within a stifling room. They were a bit startled when the tiles across the roof had begun to shift, pulled aside by eager hands above their heads. Then, a pallet began to descend, a withered man clutching the ragged edges, trembling as his body sank toward the heads of the crowd below. Some of the crowd called for the men above to cease lowering their burden while others began to push their neighbors aside to make room for the paralytic. Some of the crowd eased through the doorway, to make room for the pallet as it came to rest before Jesus. The man on the pallet uneasily glanced from person to person, seldom making eye contact in his uneasiness at usurping space in the crowded room. And then his glance came to the one his friends had sought. And he stopped, gazing in hope at this man.

Jesus knelt, looking at him for a moment, then said, "Son, your sins are forgiven."

Silence held the room still for a moment. Then a small pent up sigh escaped an older man seated to one side of Jesus. The eyes of the crowd turned in his direction, expecting more. But he sat there, his eyes on the ground as he fingered the heavy fringe of his garment.

Jesus looked at him, then looked at the other leaders seated along the edge of the crowd. They had been present all day, listening to his teaching, their posture stiffly indicating their lack of pleasure at the crowd's careful attention to the teaching of this man.

"Why are you thinking these things?" Jesus asked the leaders. "Which is easier to say to this paralyzed man, 'Your sins are forgiven,' or to say 'Get up, take your mat and walk'?

The crowd considered this along with the leaders. Small murmurs across the crowded room indicated which was the more likely possibility. The leaders said nothing. It was a loaded question in their intractable opposition to this teacher.

Turning back, to the man on the pallet, Jesus added, "But that you may know that the Son of Man has authority on earth to forgive sins," he paused as he briefly looked at the religious leaders. Turning back to the paralyzed man, he ordered. "I tell you, get up, take your mat, and go home!" [3]

Before the startled eyes of the crowd, the man rolled to one side and then rose to his knees, before climbing to his feet. Briefly he swayed, grasping for balance. He rolled up the mat and pushed his way through the crowded room. The silence was broken by a murmur and then someone laughed. Soon the crowd was pushing from the room, following the man Jesus had just healed, calling to those they passed. They pointed at the former paralytic striding along the road, carrying his mat. And they praised God.

The men now sharing this Passover meal with Jesus

had been present, watching the former paralytic rise up to make his way out of the crowded room. They had heard their leader forgive the man for the sins he had committed against God. So as they sat over their Passover meal, it did not seem strange to hear Jesus proclaim forgiveness for their sins. They remained uncertain exactly how his blood could be poured out as part of a covenant with God when they watched him bite into another piece of bread. Here he sat, among them, living, breathing. They did not anticipate the storm about to break over the city of Jerusalem with Jesus' arrest.

For the disciples, the bread and wine, were a matter of eating and drinking for physical sustenance. Even with the mental imagery of the sacrificial lamb and the events centuries before as the Angel of Death passed over those hidden beneath the blood, they could not fathom the significance of Jesus' words. They did not grasp the imagery of his body as bread broken for them, his blood as wine shed for their sins. His words contained echoes of the Passover tradition as the blood of a sacrifice was a central theme in the history of the Jews' deliverance from bondage. For the disciples that was ancient history though they had witnessed the sacrifices taking place in the temple courtyard and the blood from animal sacrifice staining the altar daily.

In three years of ministry, as Jesus taught those who followed him, he frequently used examples from daily life that allowed those who listened to grasp what he was teaching. God has communicated with man from the very beginning of time by giving us physical examples of what he wishes us to understand. As Jesus taught his disciples on the last evening he would spend with them before going to the cross, he chose the most common elements of a meal set before them. Bread and wine.

Bread had long been a staple in the diet of the tribes along the Mediterranean Sea. As the tribal peoples began to give up a nomadic life style, centered around hunting and the flocks of domesticated animals, their reliance on what could be grown year after year became the basis of their society. The Jewish people were now an agrarian society, raising crops of wheat and barley, which were ground into course flour. Bread sustained the men as they worked in the fields. Bread fed their hungry children. Depending on a crop that could be renewed year after year allowed the tribes to grow, supporting a larger population than they might once have done when depending on what could be brought back from hunting. Bread was essential to sustaining life.

But in the death of an animal, these people understood that life was sustained in the blood pumping through their veins. With a heritage of raising domesticated animals, men understood that once an animal's blood began to flow from its veins, life slipped away. In Leviticus 17:11, Moses had taught the Jewish people,

> *"For the life of a creature is in the blood,*
> *and I have given it to you to make atonement*
> *for yourselves on the altar; it is the blood that*
> *makes atonement for one's life."*

In a primitive society where an accident could steal a loved one from his family so quickly with little to be done, these men understood the significance of blood being the life flow. As they witnessed the sacrifices, their hands on the head of the sacrifice, they understood the animal carried their shame before God.

Jesus picked up the loaf of bread and spoke of his body being broken. These men could see his hands breaking apart the loaf and visualize the hands of a violent man ripping apart flesh. They could visualize the red stain of wine spilled across a table as the blood seeping from one's veins. At that moment they did not understand that Jesus was speaking of his own death just hours away. But in time they did see the picture of sacrifice and this image would haunt each of them for the remainder of their lives as they spoke of Jesus' sacrifice on our behalf.

We, the condemned, have been pardoned by the perfect sacrifice stepping into our place to be broken and torn. Without blood there is no forgiveness for sin.[4] Jesus shed his blood to cover our sin. Eleven of these twelve men would associate the image of broken bread, the sip of wine with the image of Jesus hanging on a cross. They taught those who believed their message to remember Jesus' sacrifice as we meet together. We are all recipients of God's great grace, binding us into a body of believers, eagerly anticipating the return of the one who paid the price for our redemption.

Centuries earlier, an ancient covenant was written in the blood of a sacrifice, granting the recipient an annual pardon from God's judgement. Jesus' words on that evening as he spoke of "the blood of the new covenant" would become vitally clear to the apostles. The Abrahamic covenant, followed by the Mosaic covenant, had come down through the patriarchs to the Jews of the first century. These covenants between God and man were written first in the blood of animals. But with his death the blood of one man, Christ Jesus, initiated a new contract between God and man. A contract that overrode all others. Just as Jesus' hands tore apart the essential ingredient for physical life, his blood sealed the covenant that offers us life in an eternal relationship with Jesus, the righteous one.

We are now two thousand years removed from that shadowy evening. Our culture does not reflect the agrarian roots that formed the foundation of life for Jesus' followers. Recently, as I talked about this topic with a friend, I asked her what she thought about during Communion.

"I guess I try to think about his sacrifice for me, about how it was for Jesus to hang on the cross, all his suffering. But," she admitted, "I get distracted. I can only think about it so much before I find I'm going over the same thoughts again and again."

I've thought that many of us, in our more honest moments, would echo that sentiment. For many years, I found myself struggling to identify with the suffering of Jesus as he hung on the cross. But it was too far removed from my own experience. The society we live in insulates us from pain, from one's life leaking from some horrendous wound into the dust beneath our feet. I haven't lived with whips or crowns of thorns. How could I come to understand the significance of Communion when I face God across the plate of starchy wafers?

In order to understand the significance of what we have undertaken, let us look back in time at an ancient contract, a fading image written in blood. And then, we will look a little deeper at our commitment and how it evolves into the larger context of the body of Christ. Let us examine what it means to share the joys and the sorrows that come to us through entering a contract with the living God.

You see, when we meet over Communion, we accept the privilege of sharing in the sorrow and the joy that are in Christ. When we turn our backs on Communion, we not only reject a sacrament but we leave behind a rich heritage represented in the living, breathing souls that make up Christ's body. As we consider the sacrament that Jesus left his followers, let us begin with the concept of a covenant between God and man.

Chapter 2

The Covenant

Dusk settled across the encampment, the last remnants of light creeping over the rock outcroppings that littered the brown plain. The upper most branches of the largest trees seemed to seize the last shred of light, before releasing it to the dim glow that muted the subtle features of the landscape surrounding the camp. Then, even the dim glow was snuffed out, leaving the night pitch black, lit only by a large campfire at the edge of the tents. Dust, mixed with acrid smoke, swirled through the encampment, holding the tents in a black haze. Mothers hushed the voices of their children at play. Dogs crept beneath the loose folds of tents, their eyes all that shone in the reflection of a red glare from the fire.

Three visitors had entered the encampment earlier that day. At their approach, Abraham rose from his seat beneath the ancient trees that marked Mamre. He graciously invited the three men to sit while the women moved to quickly prepare food and drink for the visitors. His dark eyes examined the men's clothing and their bearing as they moved confidently into the shade of the trees to settle on rugs spread over the dusty ground. Abraham called for water, offering the men refreshment in washing the dust from feet, hands and faces. The women kneaded bread dough near primitive stone ovens. The voice of a calf bawling was cut short as blood flowed from it's severed veins. Male servants soon roasted large cuts of meat.

As Abraham watched his visitors, he sensed that they were not of human descent. This would not be the first time he had stood in the presence of the almighty God. His eldest servants could remember the solid mud structures of Haran, the town that last sheltered Abraham before he embarked on a journey to this remote plain. He had been relatively well off by the standards of Haran.

In Haran, Abraham claimed that a Spirit, unseen by human eyes, was calling him to leave his home built with mud bricks for a nomadic life in a tent, following great herds of sheep and goats. This Spirit had promised to make his descendants a great nation, powerful throughout the earth. Those that cursed his descendants would find the curse returned upon them. Those who blessed Abraham's descendants would be blessed in return.

After his departure from Haran, the man, then named Abram, continued to live a nomadic life style until the day when this same Spirit had come to him once again.

Watching his three visitors, Abraham recalled that earlier time when he had entered a covenant with the Spirit he now obeyed. He had seemed restless that day, moving through the tents, discontent with the daily routine. Something was troubling him. Settling into the rugs that made his bed, Abram slept, crying out as his dream moved him. When he woke, he moved quickly toward the herds of cattle, sheep and goats, selecting one of each animal. He called for his men to bring the heifer he had chosen along with a dove and pigeon. Settling around the campfire, the men watched as Abram pulled out a long sharp knife, drawing it against the mighty arteries hidden in the corded necks of each animal. As the blood stained the dust around them, Abram struggled to slice each animal in half, leaving only the two birds whole.

Throughout that afternoon, he sat with the carcasses spread around him, driving off the vultures that were drawn by the smell of blood. Flicking his hands at the flies that clustered over the decaying carcasses, he waited as dusk settled over the campsite. As he fell into a deep sleep, a dim glow shone out of the darkness as if an obscure form moved through the stinking meat and blood, carrying a pot of coals. Smoke swirled in the passage as a flame shot up from the coals. The darkness seemed to hold a physical presence and Abram groaned as if in pain and misery. His men froze in place, afraid to move, afraid that the physical weight of this unseen presence would overwhelm them, driving them into the dust. For hours they hugged the ground in fear, in obeisance to the unseen presence until Abram rose from his position near the campfire to summon them closer.

Out of the darkness God had spoken to Abram, chaning his name to Abraham, the father of a multitude. He had promised that the descendants of this man would inherit the land Abraham roamed. And yet, there was still no heir to begin even the slimmest line of descendants reaching into immortality.

Now Abraham, as he had been called since the day of the covenant, waited for his three visitors to reveal why they had come to his camp. The older servants shook their heads. Sarah, Abraham's wife, moved slowly through the encampment, no longer of child bearing age. Her gray hair a symbol of the long years she had followed this man, Abraham. Years had passed as the men followed the herds. The night of glowimg embers was a dim memory.

Abraham watched as his visitors tasted his bread and the sizzling roast placed before them. Yet, he sensed that receiving his hospitality was not their goal in visiting his camp.

Breaking the silence, one of the men inquired as to Abraham's health. "God has blessed me with good health," he replied, still waiting.

"And Sarah, where is she," the visitor asked.

Abraham could hear the slightest giggle from one of Sarah's servants. "She is back in the tent," he said, nodding toward the dusty form rising toward the branches above. He could imagine how Sarah strained to hear the mention of her name.

"When I return next year, she will have given you a son."

The visitor smiled, watching Abraham's struggle between elation and doubt. Turning his head slightly to look at the tent, the visitor asked, "Why does Sarah laugh? Why does she believe that this is too hard for God?"

Hidden in the tent, Sarah cringed back against the rugs. She had not made a sound as amusement filled her at the visitor's words. How could he have known that she silently laughed at this announcement? She was too old to become pregnant. Her body had betrayed her. She no longer bled monthly. Her time was past. Fear crept into her. How could this visitor have heard her doubt, unspoken but creasing throughout her consciousness?

A year later, Sarah presented a son, Isaac, to Abraham. With the fulfillment of his promise, God gave flesh to his covenant with Abraham. The covenant was more

than a promise to bless an ancient patriarch with an heir. Abraham's descendants would become a mighty nation, inhabiting land that spread from the rolling waves of the Mediterranean to the valley of the Jordan River, from the great cedars of Lebanon to the desert sands of the Negev. Their influence would spread throughout every culture as Abraham's descendants were disseminated throughout the nations on six
continents.

A covenant! God, the Almighty stepped down to the level of his creation to make an agreement with the created. For centuries, men designed their own gods out of wood and stone. Then, a man, Abraham, spoke of a God without human form, a Spirit. This eternal God existed before time, sovereign over all the universe. Yet, God did not leave man to exist as created apart from him. Our creator sought communication with us. He chose to enter into a covenant, a sacred contract, with Abraham. He promised to bless Abraham and in return, he asked Abraham to trust him for a son. That covenant between God and man can be summed up in one brief statement, quoting Genesis 17:1b.

"I am God almighty; walk before me and be blameless."

Long before Abram walked the streets of Ur, man had walked with God in a beautiful garden. Though he was blessed in a relationship with the creator and sustainer of the Universe, man was not satisfied. He disobeyed the one command God had given him. That first man failed to walk blameless, choosing to disobey his creator. His disobedience separated him and his descendants from God.

Now, the descendants of that first man had a second chance. Through Abraham, God promised a savior to mankind. Michael Lawler, a scholar of Jewish Law, tells us the term for making a covenant is *likhrot berit*, meaning to *cut a covenant*. 1 The term came out of an ancient ritual in which an animal was cut in half. The two parties making the covenant walked together between the two halves as part of their agreement. The two halves were then tied together, symbolizing the unity between the two parties. This helps us understand why Abram cut the animals in half and stood watch as he waited for God to come and join in the covenant. Death was a part of the covenant-making process. Old agreements were set aside in order to form a new covenant.

With this new covenant God and Abraham, two separate entities, were bonded together. Mankind had not seen this close bond between creator and created since Adam had fallen, breaking the first covenant. As his sign of a new covenant, God chose circumcision, or the cutting of the foreskin. Though he was advancing in years, Abram underwent circumcision and required this of all the men under his authority. God then changed his name to Abraham, meaning the father of many nations. The old was cut away, the new covenant emerged. This covenant was renewed with each successive generation. Unlike a contract in a business agreement, a covenant is sacred, in the past requiring the shedding of blood to seal the accord between two parties. God was making an irrevocable promise to Abraham and his descendents.

Years after Abraham's death, when his chosen people became slaves in Egypt, God raised a leader, Moses, to bring his people out of slavery. On the eve of their departure, God required a blood sacrifice to preserve life. That blood was spread on the lintel and doorposts of each house as a covering, protecting those gathered inside. The Jewish people could not miss the covenant agreement with their God as they stared at the blood splattered across the doorposts.

Moses, their leader, reminded them in Exodus 24:8, *"This is blood of the covenant, which God has commanded you to keep."*

Upon departing Egypt, God gave his chosen people a system of laws as part of that covenant to protect them against evil. In Deuteronomy 28, verses 1-2 and 15, Moses, their leader, promised the descendants of Abraham,

"If you fully obey the Lord your God and carefully follow all his commands I give you today, the Lord your God will set you high above all the nations on earth.
All these blessings will come upon you and accompany you if you obey the Lord your God."
"However, if you do not obey the Lord your God and do not carefully follow all his commands and decrees I am giving you today, all these curses will come upon you and overtake you."

The agreement at Mount Sinai became known as the Mosaic or Sinai covenant. Each year, the Israelite men brought their sacrifice to the tabernacle, followed later by the temple. Each man stepped up to the altar to present his sacrifice to God. The man laid his hand upon the animal's head offering the animal as a sacrifice for the sins this man had committed in the previous twelve months. With the sacrifice completed, the man or woman could walk free for another year, at peace with God. Yet each year, the sacrifice must be repeated. The man returned to the altar, leading his sacrifice. No animal conceived in a world infected by sin could be a perfect sacrifice as remission for all time for the sins of the penitent.

Under the old covenant, Abraham's descendants were given a system of laws that defined how they could live and how they could apply for God's blessing in their lives. This was sealed in blood by the sacrifices offered under the stipulation of the Covenant. Yet, in those sacrifices, if they chose to live outside the law, they could incur God's wrath and bring down cursing on their individual lives and that of the nation.

In looking at the history between God and the ancient nation of Israel, from the time of Moses, we see the covenant binding both God and Israel. This agreement was more than a simple contract with each party retaining certain conditions. Unlike a contract, this covenant was a sacred agreement with a holy God, based on love. A covenant based on God's love for his people. Rather than a financial agreement, a covenant springs from the sacred, drawing us into worship of our creator and Savior. This covenant gives both parties a role to fulfill.

Today, as people called by the name of Christ, we live under God's grace. Yet, we still experience the same concept as once governed Israel: If we fulfill the terms of our covenant with God, he will bless us in one form or another. When we ignore our covenant with God, we risk God's discipline in our lives. If we are held to such a weighty agreement let us examine the meaning, the terms of the covenant.

Our covenant with God today does not involve the shedding of blood each and every year. God sent his own son as the unblemished sacrifice to die for our sins. At the moment Jesus hung between heaven and earth, his blood spilling into the dust of Golgotha, our debt was paid for all time. The Bible tells us that with Jesus' death, "the curtain of the temple was torn in two from top to bottom." No longer was a division between God and man necessary. 2

> *"When Christ came as high priest of the good things that are already here, he went through the greater and more perfect tabernacle that is not man-made, that is to say, not a part of this creation.*
> *He did not enter by means of the blood of goats and calves; but he entered the Most Holy Place once for all by his own blood, having obtained eternal redemption. The blood of goats and bulls and the ashes of a heifer sprinkled on those who are ceremonially unclean sanctify them so that they are outwardly clean. How much more, then, will the blood of Christ, who through the eternal Spirit offered himself unblemished to God, cleanse our consciences from acts that lead to death, so that we may serve the living God!"* Hebrews 9:11-14

No more carcasses bleeding out into the dust. The old covenant that required the blood of a sacrifice had been satisfied. The new covenant between God and man was now written in the blood of a perfect lamb, Jesus Christ. The one who stood perfect in God's sight had been sacrificed in order to declare a new covenant between God and man, based on the blood of Jesus Christ. In that moment, our perception of God changed. He had been the God of the Law. Now, he is the God of Love. His sacrifice came out of his great love for us.

When Jesus came as the final perfect sacrifice, he fulfilled the old covenant. His sacrifice, on our behalf, met all the requirements for us to become righteous by taking our unrighteousness upon himself. This was sealed in his blood. Through his blood we seek forgiveness for every wrong we have committed and will commit in the future.

Ancient people, those of Abraham's time, understood that life itself flowed through the blood. When an artery was opened the blood flowed out. Without blood, the body could no longer sustain life. To seal a covenant with blood, was to give it the utmost importance. Christ's blood shed for us gives us life. With the old covenant fulfilled, a new covenant was called for, extending to all people, not just the blood descendants of Abraham.

Jesus, the one who shed his blood for us, is called the mediator of the new covenant. A mediator acts as a intermediary between two parties, the parties that have joined in a covenant. With his bloodshed, Jesus defines the terms of the covenant between God and man. He did this out of love for his creation, purchasing mankind from the tyranny of sin. 3

Now take a moment to transfer the concept behind the old covenant to this new covenant that stands between us and God as stated in Matthew 26:27b-28,

> *"Drink from it, all of you. This is my blood of the covenant, which is poured out for the forgiveness of sins."*

And again in I Corinthians 11, *"This is the new covenant in my blood, do this, whenever you drink it, in remembrance of me."*

We have a new covenant, established at the time of

Jesus's death. Yet, echoes of the old covenant remain as part of our legal system, forming the foundation of what is expected from us today.

> God promised under the new covenant,
> *"I will put my laws in their hearts. I will be their God, and they will be my people. No longer will a man teach his neighbor or a man his brother, saying, 'Know the Lord,' because they will all know me, from the least of them to the greatest. For I will forgive their wickedness and will remember it no more."*
>
> *By calling this covenant 'new,' he has made the first one obsolete; and what is obsolete and aging will soon disappear."* Hebrews 8:9-12

By placing God's law in our conscience, the echoes of the old covenant become the foundation of the new covenant. As we learn from the teaching of the New Testament, we come to understand our need to come to God and confess our sin. The redeeming work of God's spirit enables us to repent of our sin. In return, God's word promises:

> *"If we confess our sins, God is faithful to forgive us those sins and cleanse us from all unrighteousness."*
> I John 1:9

This is the new covenant in simple terms. God promises forgiveness when we confess our sins, placing his righteousness on us.

As Jesus broke bread and sipped the wine the night before his final sacrifice, he gave his disciples two visual elements and a time of reflection to consider the terms of his covenant with them. His blood in exchange for forgiveness, for life. As he broke the loaf of bread, Jesus called on his disciples to, in time, use the sacraments of bread and wine to remember his sacrifice. But then the Apostle Paul adds a further stipulation.

> *"A man ought to examine himself before he eats of the bread and drinks of the cup.*
> *For anyone who eats and drinks without recognizing the body of the Lord, eats and drinks judgement on himself."* I Corinthians 11:28-29

This is what is required under the new covenant. We stop! We have come to the altar, God's altar, the place we meet with the Almighty creator, the one who sustains our very lives.

The Israelites were instructed:

> *"No man should appear before the Lord empty-handed: Each of you must bring a gift in proportion to the way the Lord your God has blessed you."*
> Deuteronomy 17:16b-17

Think about this for a moment. We so casually call upon God when we are frightened or lonely, heartsick over wrong-doing. What do we bring to the altar as our sacrifice, as a gift to our redeemer?

Under the new covenant, we recognize that we are called to lay our lives, our will, every action before God. Before we take the bread and the wine at Communion, we are called to examine our lives and actions. We confess our sin, renewing communion with God. Only then do we participate in the sacrament of Communion. Without repentence we dishonor the sacrifice that Jesus made for us. If we ignore the call to self examination and repentence, we seem to regard Jesus' sacrifice as of little consequence in our lives today.

Many of us in the North American church have become complacent in our remembrance of Christ's death through the sacrament of communion. We sit in our padded seats and pass the sacramental elements. Our minds are caught by the demands of our busy lives. We may have become complacent as we celebrate this sacrament year in, year out. The sacrament has lost the primacy in Christian faith that would become so vivid if we were to catch a glimpse of life spilling into the dust. We've forgotten that this is a covenant between us and the Almighty God, the God who does not take our commitment lightly. We are to live the reality of this covenant moment by moment of each day.

In our litigious society, we fear the expense and consequences of legal action. Somehow, we do not attach the same fear to the consequences of breaking our covenant with God. We do not see him hauling us into court, stabbing an accusing finger in our face as we huddle in fear before a stern faced judge. Yet the consequences of failing to honor our covenant with God reach far further than monetary loss or the forfeiting of physical freedom. Failure warps our very soul, separating us from God.

If I seem to be making more of this commitment than is warranted, let me take you to the other side, to Satan's contract with those he enslaves. In his book, *The Twilight Labyrinth*, George Otis Jr., explores the contracts that

---

* *The Twilight Labyrinth by George Otis, Jr., is available from The Sentinel Group @ SentinelGroup.org.*

tribal people throughout the world have made with the demons that rule the geographical locations they reside in. He traces that history back in time to the years that followed the ancient story of the Tower of Babel.*

The occupants of Babel, their once common language disrupted into a multitude of tongues, began to leave the vast plain that once was the center of their building program. Caravans, loaded with possessions, dispersed in different directions. The author, George Otis, writes:

"The experiences of Babel's outbound tribes were as varied as their tongues and destinations. But a careful examination of history reveals at least one important common denominator. At one point or another along their long march, each of these ancient peoples encountered some form of collective trauma.

Regardless of whether Satan caused these circumstances or simply took advantage of them, their effect was to provide him a direct entré into the psyches of otherwise distracted people. It was a perfect setup. Not only did the trauma provoke open discussion of supernatural powers, it also prompted distraught souls to call on these powers.

By posing as golden age deities capable of delivering the community from their present ordeal, demonic agents lured a desperate general populace into long-term quid pro quo pacts. The deal was simple. In return for allegiance pledged to these masquerading demons, the community would receive immediate trauma relief as well as restored access to the power, wisdom and deities of their forefathers.

As to the nature or source of the traumas that precipitated these pacts, history records at leave five notable phenomena.

1. Intimidating natural barriers;
2. Climatic and natural disasters;
3. Disease and pestilence;
4. Famine and environmental ruin;
5. Wars and raids." 4

He continues,

"We cannot construct the details of every pact that has welcomed demonic forces into the human community, but this does not mean these contracts are speculative. In many instances, quality documentation does exist - and when the evidence is examined, a compelling and consistent pattern emerges.

What we see is this: After an initial bargain is struck, almost always under circumstantial duress, demons proceed to prove themselves by providing the community or individual with a measure of trauma relief. In some situations the relief is real; in others it is simply a cleverly administered placebo. Whether real or imagined, however, the onset of recovery signals that it is time to pay the piper.

Most commonly, debt servicing on such pacts is accomplished through some form of ritual tribute or public allegiance - and the 'interest' (rate) can be brutal. Those who fail to read the contractual fine print up-front are often distressed to learn that they have obligated themselves to long-term and radically one-sided arrangements. When this reality sinks in, they become prisoners of fear and despair. If they default on their part of the bargain, they risk inviting a recurrence of the original trauma. If they honor the pact, they remain subject to the powers and capricious temperament of their new master." 5

Otis goes on to describe several examples of particular people groups who remained enslaved to these pacts with demonic powers, dating back over centuries of time. The first involves a people group in India.

"In his outstanding book Eternity in Their Hearts, veteran missionary and author Don Richardson recounts the circumstances of another ancient pact-making crisis, this one involving the ancestors of India's Santal people. After a long eastward migration, these early wayfarers suddenly found their way blocked by the imposing Hindu Kush Mountains in northeastern Afghanistan. Trapped in this treacherous terrain, the weaker members began to grow faint. Lack of sustenance and unpredictable weather conditions became serious concerns. Concluding that their progress was being impeded by powerful mountain spirits known as Maran Buru, the tribal elders decided to proffer a quid pro quo pact. 'O Maran Buru,' they covenanted, 'if you release a pathway for us, we will bind ourselves to you when we reach the other side.' Centuries later, in 1867, two Scandinavian missionaries encountered the Santal people living in a region north of Calcutta, India. They were puzzled as to why the Santal word for demons translated as 'spirits of the mountains,' since there were no mountains in the immediate vicinity. The mystery was solved when an esteemed Santal elder named Kolean filled in the final details of his ancestors' journey through the Hindu Kush.

"After covenanting with the Maran Buru,' he explained,' they came upon a passage in the direction of the rising sun.' This opening, which may have been the famous Khyber Pass, they named Bain, or 'Day Gate.' Emerging onto the plains of the Indian subcontinent, the relieved tribe fulfilled their oath by practicing spirit appeasement." [6]

In another example, Otis relates a horrible story - I'll skip the details - of a five year-old Chilean shepherd boy being sacrificed by an old shamaness after a tsunami in 1960 to appease the spirits of an angry sea. Such a sacrifice would seem out of place in modern times. The pact behind the sacrifice was very old.

On the continent of Africa, a missionary in Kenya has told me of a similar agreement. When questioned about why the tribal people continue certain tradition in their everyday lives, the response is that it is due to a covenant made by their ancestors with the spirits that rule their region. A simple statement with great spiritual consequence.

In reviewing the contracts that Satan has established with tribal people all over our planet, it becomes obvious that our spiritual commitment is not something to take lightly. Under the dominion of Satan's minions, tribes, even nations, have been trapped in superstition and fear. Their corrupt leaders do not hesitate to turn the superstitions to their own benefit, often leaving their subjects impoverished with no hope for the future. Fear, poverty and souls caught in bondage are all hallmarks of Satan's dominion. He is unwilling to release any subject he holds under contract. Whole nations and people groups have been held in bondage since ancient times based on a contract their forefathers signed in blood. This is far removed from the legal maneuvering that takes place in our legal system today.

A spiritual battle is raging on our planet. On one side we have those who serve God and who fall under a covenant, undergirded by love and grace. The opposition also holds adherents to a contract - I will not say covenant as there is nothing sacred about an agreement with demonic forces. There is no middle ground. Which will we choose? As we consider that question, we need to see the fading, brown letters of an ancient contract truly written in blood.

Having examined the covenant the creator offers us, I would ask two questions.

Am I willing to enter into a covenant with God?

Will I keep the stipulations of such a covenant to the final letter?

Webster's Dictionary defines a contract as "an agreement between two or more people to do something, especially one set forth in writing and enforceable by law, a compact, a covenant."

Generally a contract states the obligations on the part of each party in an agreement, committing them to complete a set of actions. The rewards and the consequences of fulfilling the agreement or the failure to do so become part of the legal agreement.

So it is with God in his covenant with believers. When we come to God, in sorrow and repentence, we are seeking forgiveness for our sins. As we seek forgiveness, we enter into a holy covenant with him. For his part, he loves us as his creation. He forgives us all our wrong doing and imparts his righteousness to us. We stand before him clean and forgiven.

We are granted a fresh start. We are no longer required to bring an animal sacrifice as the ancient Israelites did each year at Passover. We place ourselves under the dominion of our Lord. We become his sons and daughters, his heirs to all the attributes he possesses. We learn to love Him.

In submitting to God, we are not left alone. The Spirit of God is speaking to us constantly, reminding us of the covenant that we have with our creator and Savior, reminding us of the great love he has shown for us. God has imputed his righteousness to us. Now, he guides us in our decisions and comforts us when we fail to live up to expectations. We no longer struggle to live good lives on our own. We no longer feel inadequate in difficult decisions. We have a guide.

What is expected on our part? Now, that is the challenging part of the pact for us. Simply said, we are human. We are called to set aside all unrighteousness and to live Godly lives. We are to set aside our own wills and allow God to work through us. No longer do we have a right to make decisions without consulting God. Every part of our life must come under his Lordship: Attitudes, speech, our thoughts, our actions. Everything!

This is not about a rigid system of rules. Human beings seem to take comfort in defining a relationship with God by setting out rules governing behavior. While the law of the Old Testament still echoes in our legal system today, our behavior is restrained by our love for God under the new covenant. With Jesus we have come to know the God who loves us, who would send his son to take our place. In turn, we learn to love God as we share a daily discourse with him.

This is the reality of the covenant that we have with God. He promises forgiveness and his righteousness. We promise to make him Lord of our lives turning from all unrighteousness. I am reminded of this covenant every time I take Communion because I am reminded of what he gave for me. As I sink my teeth into the bread and swallow the wine, I am renewing that covenant. As I commemorate the shedding of Jesus' blood for me, I am pledging myself anew to the terms of the covenant.

Without Communion, I fear that we begin to take this covenant too lightly. The elements of bread and wine are familiar, something we live with day in, day out. When we come to the Communion service we are busy people, we are tempted to rush through the time to examine ourselves. We think we will deal with this examination more thoroughly when we have time. But that time never quite comes. There is always something more urgent to settle. As a result our covenant with God suffers from neglect.

Let's take that thought out of the context of our modern culture. In the next chapter let me introduce you to the Shuar people of the jungles of eastern Ecuador.

Chapter 3

Committed

Years ago, I stood in the door of the church, watching a line of Shuar men and women, in groups of three and four, straggle down the dirt path toward the buildings of the mission station in the eastern jungles of Ecuador. The men were dressed in simple trousers and shirts, the women in colorful dresses pieced from contrasting prints of colorful fabrics. Most were barefoot, their toes splayed against the red clay, the soles of their feet as tough as leather. Leaving the church building, they strolled companionably toward the center of community commerce.

Each Sunday, the members of the tribe walked out of the surrounding jungle, along muddy paths, to congregate in the church building which stood along a narrow strip of grass that served as a runway. The planes of Mission Aviation Fellowship flew supplies into the isolated station from the central base located thirty minutes from the edge of civilization. The station, enclosed by dense jungle, centered around a school and a store with supplies stacked on shelves of raw wood. The homes of the missionaries were set further back from the airstrip, forming a small community.

At one time, the group of believers and missionaries had met in a traditional lodge made of chonta palm and bamboo. The open door allowed small farm animals and pets to wander among the dusty streaks of sunlight that filtered through the bamboo slats across the packed dirt floor. The congregation gathered on narrow wooden benches, beneath a thatched roof, listening to the speaker. Native hymns, some with melodies familiar to North American visitors, drifted into the open air.

In time, the station acquired a small sawmill and produced enough lumber to build a modern structure with rough planks forming the walls and floor. The roof was of corrugated tin, the windows remained without glass, open to rain or flying insects. The congregation sat on narrow wood benches that included a plank across the back, somewhat more comfortable than the benches of the traditional lodge I had encountered when my family moved to the station.

The service began with music, each song in three waves. The girls of the mission school sang a little faster than the body of the congregation while those less familiar with the music lagged slightly behind. One of the resident missionaries or a native leader of the church might give the message. A second speaker might tag on to the message, delivering a homily for some moments before a final prayer dismissed the congregation for the day. This routine varied on Sundays when Communion was served. Before the final prayer, an invitation would be extended for all to stay that were willing to take Communion after a fifteen minute break in the service.

On that Sunday, I stood at the entrance to the church, as nearly three quarters of the congregation drifted down the mud path toward the the school and the lawn surrounding the store. Only a handful of believers and missionaries stayed for the observance of the Lord's Supper.

Communion, the sacrament of bread and wine commemorating Jesus's death, was not a new concept to the Shuar. The missionaries had carefully instructed the first converts in this sacrament, based on scriptural teaching.

> *"Therefore, whoever eats the bread or drinks the cup of the Lord in an unworthy manner will be guilty of sin ning against the body and blood of the Lord. A man ought to examine himself before he eats of the bread and drinks of the cup. For anyone who eats and drinks without recognizing the body of the Lord eats and drinks judgement on himself. That is why many among you are weak and sick, and a number of you have fallen asleep. But if we judged ourselves, we would not come under judgement. When we are judged by the Lord, we are being disciplined so that we will not be condemned with the world."*   I Corinthians 11:27-32

In the 1960's, the Shuar remained a primitive people, animistic belief pervading tribal ritual. Only a few years before, the practice of head shrinking had been actively practiced by the men of the tribe. The spare number of middle-aged men remained out of proportion to population numbers. It was not uncommon for the men to have several wives, marrying girls as young as ten years of age. Social gatherings included drinking a fermented mixture of yucca root, the resulting activity rarely conducive to growth in Christian principles. Through teaching God's word, the missionaries had begun to make inroads into animistic belief and cultural practices but the struggle remained intense. These people understood that to take up the cross of Christ, involved setting aside much of their cultural practices. Head shrinking was definitely out. Men could have only one wife and had to live in social and spiritual harmony with their neighbors.

Every believer is called to examine himself before partaking of Communion. To do so forces us to examine whether our lives are in line with scriptural teaching. I Corinthians 11:28 instructs a man to examine himself on where he stands with God before taking the sacrament that represents the sacrifice of Jesus on our behalf.

To the Shuar, blood and sacrifice were a very real part of their culture. They all knew men who had unwisely strolled down a path from their lodges, only to have their head separated from their shoulders. To honor Christ's sacrifice required a sacrifice of their own. They had to give up many cultural practices that had existed long before their birth. This required some thought. It was not something to be taken lightly. A fifteen-minute interval was granted for social leave taking, for appointment making, to step aside from one's culture. A commitment was required. Where does one stand on the body and blood of Christ?

> I Corinthians states, *"For anyone who eats and drinks without recognizing the body of the Lord eats and drinks judgement on himself."*

What does the Bible mean by recognizing the body of the Lord? To understand this we must look at the sacrifice that Jesus made in his death on earth.

We view life as precious. When illness or accident strikes, threatening our lives, we fight to hang onto every breath, to extend our lives by just a few more moments. In God's view, life is transitory, a passing from a conscious earthly presence into eternity. For a Christian, living in the daily attendance to God, we can look forward to standing in God's presence for eternity when our lives here on earth are finished. In that perspective, we understand that death was not the final moment for Jesus as he hung on the cross.

Jesus' agony came from the weight of sin that permeated his last moments as he took our guilt upon himself. For one who had known only righteous perfection, the stench of evil, the corruption that entangled his spirit was beyond our knowledge of endurance. God, the Father, turned away. He could not look at Jesus as he hung between heaven and earth, a sacrifice for their creation. Jesus' death was the only way that we could come before God and stand in his presence, both on earth and in eternity.

Communion calls us to recognize this sacrifice, to turn from sin toward the righteousnessness of God. To set aside our selfish desires, the evil that permeates our human existence and to reach for righteousness. And so we take a moment, as prescribed in I Corinthians 11 to examine ourselves. Does sin lurk in the recesses of our minds? Does it taint our approach to a righteous being, so perfect he cannot tolerate the slightest stench of sin in his presence?

Honestly, we are selfish creatures. We shrink from sacrifice, the act of putting God's righteousness before our selfish desires. The Shuar understood this. Their culture was very different from that presented through Biblical teaching. To set aside the life they had known since the first moment of birth was alien territory. In our eyes, the setting aside of their cultural practice was good. Head shrinking is not something we actively pursue. Most men in north American culture would insist that one wife, at least one wife at a time, was about all they could handle. But, in western culture, giving up private sins is much more than simply giving up a questionable practice like polygamy. The sacrifice requires us to accept God's values and priorities in place of our own. We agree to let God dictate how we act and react to what happens in life. We sacrifice our will before God.

Reflecting on the choice to give up their own desires, many Shuar chose to turn away. God had written his law upon their hearts. Instinctively, they knew what they sought out of their own interest was in conflict to that represented in a new covenant with God. Communion was a commitment to a covenant in front of their kinsman and tribal members.

Their choice? The Shuar had to accept the terms of the covenant and make a new start with God or turn their backs on the church and walk back to the life they had known.

For North Americans, this may seem a stark choice requiring little thought. But think for a moment. How often do we make that same choice within our culture?

We sit in our padded seats on Sunday mornings as the platters containing starchy wafers and cups of juice slide hand to hand along the rows. We struggle to recall and confess what has happened in the last week, the last month. In doing so, we become distracted by the demands of harried lives. Confession slides away from our consciousness as we examine some intrinsic thought that pulls us away from the righteous sacrifice represented in the blood of Christ. And then it is over. We return to our selfish priorities. We harbor offenses against one another. We have failed in our examination of ourselves. In essence, by our refusal to step aside and examine our lives under the pressure of time, we have chosen to turn our backs on what is required as we accept that wafer, that sip of juice. We have treated the sacrifice of Christ with benign indifference.

I am drawn to a passage from the prophet Malachi.

This passage is repeated several times in both the Old and New Testament.

> *"A son honors his father, and a servant his master. If I am a father, where is the honor due me, says the Lord Almighty. It is you, O priests, who show contempt for my name.*
>
> *But you ask, How have we shown contempt for your name?*
>
> *You place defiled food on my altar.*
>
> *But you ask, How have we defiled you?*
>
> *By saying that the Lord's table is contemptible. When you bring blind animals for sacrifice, is that not wrong? When you sacrifice crippled or diseased animals, is that not wrong? Try offering them to your governor! Would he be pleased with you? Would he accept you? says the Lord Almighty.*
>
> *Now implore God to be gracious to us. With such offerings from your hands, will he accept you? says the Lord Almighty.*
>
> *Oh, that you would shut the temple doors, so that you would not light useless fires on my altar! I am not pleased with you, says the Lord Almighty, and I will accept no offering from you hands."*   Malachi 1:6-10

In reading this passage, I hear God expressing both anger and grief. He is angry with the contempt for his name shown by the spiritual leaders of that day. He grieves over a creation that shows so little concern for the creator who has given them so much.

The Shuar chose to remove their physical presence from the four walls of the church building rather than contaminate the commemoration of Jesus' sacrifice by their self-willed determination to walk as they had always walked in life. Without self examination, we become calloused to God's work in our lives. We fail to grow and then wonder at the absence of God when tough times come our way.

Loneliness grows out of unmet desire for God due to the lack of time we grant him. Disconnected from God and his renewal in our lives, we wonder if we ever truly knew Him. We struggle to make decisions, privately wondering if we have failed to live to our fullest potential. For all practical purposes, we live without God under the name of Christian.

Contemplating the consequences of indifference, I want to cry out, "God, don't let this happen to me!"
I am not alone in that sentiment.

Recently, my husband asked me if I chose to catagorize sin. Sensing this was a loaded question, I gave careful consideration to my answer, and then re-phrased his question.

"Doesn't all sin separate us from God?" I asked. "I have heard some pastors say that sin of a sexual nature is more damaging to the human soul. Ultimately, I understand there are no degrees of sin as all sin separates us from God."

"The Bible teaches us that man is born with a sinful nature," he replied. "A newborn baby does not have to commit a sin to be considered a sinner before God. Just being a descendant of Adam makes me a sinner. Now how are you going to confess that during your time of self-examination before taking Communion?"

He continued by saying that we can divide sin into two categories, the sin that is inherent by being a descendant of Adam and the sin that I commit through my thoughts and actions. As I stand at the altar, before taking Communion, I'm not thinking about that moment in the garden when Satan in the sinuous form of a serpent glided up to Eve, tempting her with the fruit of the tree that God had forbidden. I'm thinking about my shortcomings that week, the times I've failed, the moments when I have deliberately set out to do wrong. I think about my actions, I search my attitudes, my mental struggles as I confess what God brings to mind. One of my favorite passages in examining my life comes from I Corinthians 13:4-7.

> *"Love is patient, love is kind. It does not envy, it does not boast, it is not proud. It is not rude, it is not self-seeking, it is not easily angered, it keeps no record of wrongs. Love does not delight in evil but rejoices in the truth. It always protects, always trusts, always hopes, always perseveres."*

How could the Apostle Paul, the writer, have known my shortcomings so well? As I contemplate my actions in light of Paul's exhortation, I find plenty to confess. In fact, I find that I had better get an early start, long before the Communion service begins. God and I have a lot to look at in the week preceding my appearance at the altar where we first signed our covenant.

I understand that God's forgiveness is for a lifetime of sin, a process we call justification. We are justified before God through Jesus' blood. Once we have been justified, the work of sanctification begins, stretching over the remainder of our lives. We are working out our salvation.

When we examine ourselves, we can only go so far before we begin to consider our actions toward other people in our discussion with God. Therein is the measure of recognizing when we are at fault and when, through sanctification, we achieve some degree of God's righteousness. God judges our hearts but our growth in Him is reflected toward other people around us.

Let's reflect back on the passage from I Corinthians. As part of this growth, I ask:

> Have I been patient today?
> Have I been kind today, all day, to others around me?
> Have I been too proud in my words and actions before others?
> Have I been rude or selfishly sought my own way?
> Have I gotten angry easily or become angry over something that I had no right to dispute?
> Have I held a grudge against another for something that person has done?
> Have I protected others, trusted them?
> Have I persevered before God to bring those whom I have encountered into a better understanding of who God is through my actions?

Every one of these questions reflects not just our relationship with God but also our relationship with other people. It is hard to recognize whether we have been kind or honest in a vacuum without the active give and take of dealing with people around us. We are called to examine ourselves. As we consider our interaction with other people, our relationship with God comes into sharp focus. We begin to realize that as we are the gift we bring to God, we have some defects just as the sacrifices God rejected at the time of the prophet, Malachi.

I Corinthians states, *"For anyone who eats and drinks without recognizing the body of the Lord eats and drinks judgement on himself."*

Without examining ourselves, without asking forgiveness for our failures as we approach the Communion table, we are no different from the people of Israel that offered defiled sacrifices before God. If we fail to address the problems in our own lives before we partake of the sacrament, we dishonor God. Can you imagine God, in total disgust, expelling man from his presence. What if he heaved one mighty breath across the palm of a hand, scattering deceit to the winds, out of his presence. The thought that he might expel me from his presence because I have failed to honor my covenant with him is terrifying. I wish to remain in the shelter of God's presence. I want to take the covenant seriously. I plead God's forgiveness for my sins.

Communion becomes a challenge to us to live our faith and this challenge goes to the heart of the covenant that we have with God. We must consider whether we will step forward to live up to the covenant or whether we will turn away. That challenge is laid down every Sunday we attend to the Communion table.

Returning to the Shuar, I recently asked a missionary who continues to serve with the tribe how the Shuar now celebrate Communion. This is the saddest part of the story.

I was told that the local church has not celebrated Communion in several years. Divisions in the local body have usurped the devotion of the local believers. The disagreements over various issues as well as the encroachment from civilization have consumed the sense of worship within the church services. The local believers are so consumed by the strife that the voice of God within many of the believers has become very quiet and hard to hear. With the local believers struggling in their relationships with each other, the church fails to be a godly example of a relationship with the almighty God before non-believers just as Israel did when they drifted away from God

    The words communion and community spring from the same root. Jesus gave us the sacrament of Communion, also called the Lord's Supper, when he shared the wine and the bread with his disciples in their last meal before his death. This was not an act he practiced alone but one that he practiced with his small community of disciples. Communion is meant to draw us into a community of believers. If we allow strife and disagreements to divide us, we lose that sense of community, the sense of unity.

    We are corporately the body of Christ, representing God's presence on earth. We cannot afford to sacrifice the sense of community to our own selfish desires. Thus, we've looked at the Communion service as a time of confession, a time to examine ourselves before God. Confession is so much more than my interaction with God. The Apostle Paul called for us to examine ourselves, to examine our actions, to examine our relationships with other people during this time. Once we have examined ourselves and asked God to forgive us, there may be more required of us. In the next chapter we will look at our role in the community of believers in the sacrament of Communion.

    Jesus said, "Do this in remembrance of me." Communion reaches beyond individual responsibility, becoming a vital sacrament to the health of the body of Christ. Let us next consider the role of confession and obedience in Communion toward building the body of Christ.

Chapter 4

A Sacrament of Living Blood

One Saturday morning I stood in a small room overlooking the auditorium of the church where I join other believers to worship God each Sunday morning. I was struck by the quiet of the sanctuary, an absolute stillness. Dim shadows filled the space. The chairs stood empty. I failed to see minute particles of dust moving in the dim beams of light that filtered through the amber tinted glass of the windows. Too quiet!

In the stillness, a spell seem to hold the auditorium captive. Unseen witnesses filled the shadows, waiting for the spell to be broken, for life to burst into the silence. At the right moment, the silence would be broken as human bodies burst through the doors like blood pumping through a heart, flowing through the rows as if they were arteries, re-animating the sanctuary back to life.

We call this building the church but in reading the Apostle Paul's letters in the New Testament, we realize that the church is made up of people rather than the building materials that form the structure. The parishioners filling the seats listen and sing, breathing life into the stillness. This is the church, the body of Christ on the planet we call Earth. The parishioners filled with warm, oxygen-rich blood bring life to a still sanctuary. Without the living, breathing souls worshiping our Lord, the building seems to ache from emptiness.

In reading the New Testament, we learn that individuals as a collective unit, form the body of Christ here on earth. The Lord's Supper plays a vital role in how this body functions. Before we look at how the sacrament of Communion effects our communities, let us consider how the body of Christ was initially formed.

In chapter two, we looked at God's relationship with Abraham. We considered the covenant that was formed between God and this patriarch, leading to a chosen nation, favored by the Creator of the universe. The Old Testament traces the history of God's interaction with this chosen people. Then, the account falls silent for four hundred years.

Two Gospels, written by Matthew, an apostle, and Luke, a physician, open the New Testament's account of Jesus' life with his birth. God was once again speaking openly to mankind as he took on the form of a tiny baby born to a woman. The Creator entered his creation. Through Jesus we would come to understand more of the sovereign God and his role in our lives. As he began his ministry, Jesus would call twelve men as disciples. These disciples would build his church by teaching others who in turn would carry Jesus' message throughout what would become Europe, western Asia and north Africa. The number of believers would grow, bringing a message down through the centuries to include the very people I anticipate bursting through the doors of the Sanctuary today.

The New Testament does not contain a definitive passage with Jesus laying out the structure and role of the church within the Christian's life, in the same way God gave his chosen people instructions on Mount Sinai. Instead we come to understand the role that the church takes in our lives through the writing of the Apostle Paul and other New Testament writers.

In Matthew 16:18, Jesus refers to the church that would come. He tells the Apostle Peter that he, Jesus, will build his church, using Peter, the 'Rock', and that the gates of hell will not stand against him. As he sent the twelve disciples out during his ministry, Jesus instructed them that whatever they would do in his name would be honored on earth and bound in Heaven.

As Jesus neared the time of his execution, he drew his disciples together with him in an upper level room to give one last time of teaching. As he spoke with them, he performed two vital services. First, he washed their feet, instructing them to do the same for each other after he was gone. In bathing their dirty feet, he offered an example of humble service to each of these men. Then, he asked them to break bread together in memory of his death and to celebrate his resurrection with a sip of wine. He gave his disciples these instructions as a corporate practice, drawing twelve individuals into one body of believers. One of these men would choose to step away in betrayal but the lesson remained. We are brought together by Christ as a body of believers representing God on earth.

The apostle John tells us Jesus taught his disciples that evening, using an analogy of branches on a vine. We cling to Jesus, his life flowing through us. At first, our focus is on our Savior. As time goes on, we begin to look around and realize that there are others who also draw their new life from Jesus. He is drawing us together, united by Him. We are dependent on Christ, the one who gives us life as just as branches receive their live clinging to the trunk of a tree.

After rising from the dead, Jesus prepared his disciples for the time when he would ascend to the Father. He instructed them to remain together in Jerusalem, awaiting the coming of His Spirit. When his Spirit came at Pentecost, the results were unforgettable. The believers burst from the room. Where they had once cowered in fear of the authorities, now they could not be contained. Filled with the power of God's Spirit, they had a message to share with the Jewish people and with the world. Before persecution drove them out of Jerusalem, Luke tells us in his account in the second chapter of Acts, verse 42, that the "believers devoted themselves to the Apostles' teaching and to the fellowship, to the breaking of bread and to prayer." This was the beginning of the church, the gathering of believers in Jesus' name, called together by the Holy Spirit. Wherever the Apostles preached, new congregations were formed and their influence remains in these regions to this day.

The church has its foundation in Christ. We are corporately called to gather together where God's word is taught by believers. We celebrate the sacraments of Communion and baptism together. Our leadership is formed under the authority of scripture. We pray, we discipline and we give together.

Once a believer professes faith in Jesus, that individual is called to be a part of a body of believers known as the body of Christ, the church. We do not function alone. The writer of the book of Hebrews tells us, "Let us not give up meeting together, as some are in the habit of doing, but let us encourage one another." [1]

The Apostle Paul wrote several key passages on the importance of each believer within the body, describing how we bring specific gifts to the other believers.

> *"The body is a unit, though it is made up of many parts: and though all its parts are many, they form one body. So it is with Christ. For we were all baptized by one Spirit into one body-whether Jews or Greeks, slave or free-and we were all given the one Spirit to drink.*
>
> *Now the body is not made up of one part but of many. If the foot should say, 'Because I am not a hand, I do not belong to the body,' it would not for that reason cease to be part of the body. And if the ear should say, 'Because I am not an eye, I do not belong to the body,' it should not for that reason cease to be part of the body. If the whole body were an eye, where would the sense of hearing be. If the whole body were an ear, where would the sense of smell be. But in fact God has arranged parts in the body, every one of them, just as he wanted them to be. If they were all one part, where would the body be. As it is there are many parts, but one body."*   I Corinthians 12: 12-20

Reading this passage, it seems clear that we are to be an active part of the body of Christ, using the gifts that God has given us. However, not all those who come to Christ are actively participating in a local Christian community. This seems to be contrary to what God has called us to do. What has happened?

We come to Jesus broken, damaged people. He forgives us and begins to heal our wounds. He allows us to grow in Him, that process stretching over the years. In the process of growing, we are called to be patient with each other. Yet, as we grow, each of us has hurt others and in turn, been hurt by others. We are not yet perfect but we are still part of the body of Christ.

Too many Christians, badly hurt by the actions of

another believer, try to remain apart from a community of Christians. When confronted, they become defensive.

"You don't know how badly I was hurt," they say. "I don't need the church."

Unfortunately, an individual who is not participating actively in a Christian community with other believers begins to falter. He is missing the vital life that flows through the corporate body just as leaves draw life from the vine. Those who remain outside the body begin to develop attitudes and actions that are not tested and refined by the support and encouragement of the corporate whole.

As I thought about an analogy to show how each believer brings something important to the body, I remembered an account I had read, written by a survivor of a Civil War battle as he struggled across the battlefield toward a field hospital.

> "I stumbled over the torn ground through the darkness between each circle of lantern light. All around the moans and cries of wounded men rose, some calling for their mothers, others toward any passing phantom. Ahead, the walls of the canvas tent that served as a field hospital inwardly glowed with lantern light. A harsh scream broke through the cries around me, a cry from the patient strapped to the table in the tent. I stumbled against a pile of debris, dropping one hand to steady myself. My hand gripped cold flesh. At that moment, the canvas wall of the tent was swept aside. The light of the lantern revealing that I had stumbled across a pile of amputated limbs. I drew back in horror."

I have taken a graphic account to use as an analogy of how a believer might be cast off when he severs his relationship with the body of Christ. He becomes a useless limb, cast off on a refuse pile, unable to fully function as God intended. He only gains value to the body of Christ when he maintains his relationship to the whole. The body of Christ needs each believer to carry out his role to the others in the body. The Apostle Paul writes in I Corinthians 12:-21-26.

> *"The eye cannot say to the hand, 'I don't need you!' On the contrary, those parts of the body that seem to be weaker are indispensable, and the parts that we think are less honorable we treat with special honor. And the parts that are unpresentable are treated with special modesty, while our presentable parts need no special treatment.*
>
> *But God has combined the members of one body and has given greater honor to the parts that lacked it, so that there should be no division in the body, but that its parts should have equal concern for each other. If one part suffers, every part suffers with it; if one part is honored, every part rejoices with it. Now you are the body of Christ, and each one of you is a part of it."*

As a body of believers, we meet together. We celebrate and worship together, we cry together. And we practice Communion together. The very root of the word *communion* shares a heritage with the word *community*. We are stronger because we are united, in spite of our differences.

Jesus knew we would need each other. Think back to the scene in Jerusalem, the week of Passover. The disciples had stumbled into the room, dusty, tired and ready to rest. They eagerly partook of the bread, the roast lamb, the wine - all of it nourishment to their bodies. Jesus did not pull each aside, breaking the bread, sharing the cup of wine with each individual. He spoke to them as a group. Communion as a sacrament was intended to be practiced together. We break the bread together, we share the wine, we serve each other.

As I have noted, divisions appear in our churches. Feelings are hurt. We cannot quite believe that someone would harm us or another person in some particular way. We draw apart, choosing to walk separately from the body of believers. We pull away from the body of Christ.

How can we break bread together as Jesus intended if we are torn apart by disagreement? We are reminded, "This is my body broken for you. Do this in remembrance of me."

With the Communion service, we are approaching the altar to offer the gift of ourselves before God. We are asked to examine ourselves: Is there a sin that needs to be confessed before we can make our offering?

As I stand at the altar or as I sit in the service celebrating Communion, I begin to examine myself. I remember that my brother has something against me. My nature is to rebel at the thought. I hate that moment!

As I discussed in the last chapter, we are born with a sinful nature. When we come to God, asking his forgiveness, he freely forgives us. Yet, we fall, again and again. I've found that if I am to confess my sin, I must do so fairly quickly or evil insidiously begins to destroy my ability to communicate with God. Confession must be kept current.

With self-examination and the command to reconcile our differences with other believers, God has granted us a great gift to build and strengthen the body. This is a process that most of us would rather forego. Many times I have worked to convince myself that a small sin will not disrupt a relationship. I tell myself that if I just ignore the break with my fellow Christian, the matter will blow over and the relationship will drift back to a normal state.

What has God asked us to do? First, we confess the sin to God and ask forgiveness. Then, based on the passage in Matthew 5, I am to leave my sacrifice at the altar. I apply this to mean that I do not take Communion but quietly sit in the service. God then instructs me to go and be reconciled to the other believer. The apostle Paul warns us that in neglecting sin in our lives, we may be guilty of "sinning against the body and the blood of our Lord."[2]

Without a doubt, this command is one of the most difficult in Scripture. I know I must humble myself in approaching my Christian brother or sister, admitting that I have been wrong. I must ask their forgiveness as I try to reconcile or make things right between us. The passage in Matthew 5 is clear that I must seek to resolve my differences with others in offering myself, holy and acceptable to God. If that should seem a little extreme, look at the covenant. We gave up control when we accepted God's forgiveness, when he imputed his righteousness to us.

God uses this process to reconcile the differences between us. Along with our private times at home, we have this time and place to meet with God as a corporate body, to examine ourselves. This process draws the church, His body, together. As divisions are healed, we are able to work and live together. The ties in the body of Christ become stronger.

My husband takes a slightly difference view of what is required. He believes that if he confesses his sin to God, he can freely take Communion and wait till after the service to approach the believer he has wronged. I am under no such illusions. I know that if I jump ahead of reconciliation in taking Communion, I am unlikely to take that step with another believer. After all, I have sought and received God's forgiveness - that is final, that is complete. If given time, I would begin to ask what more could be gained in approaching another believer other than re-opening the source of conflict. Would not such an act cause the whole disagreement to heat up once again? There could be some truth to that objection but such a statement does not go to the heart of the matter. When sin comes between two believers, the unity in the body is broken.

If I am struggling with another believer in some sort of disagreement, the conflict may disrupt more than our lives. A conflict between two believers may effect how we worship and, in time, may come to impact the body of believers to which we belong by creating divisions within the body of Christ. If we are torn apart by conflict, how can we work together? How can we celebrate together? The first instinct when conflict appears is for members of the body to go in separate directions.

God is asking us to submit everything to Him, including our pride. He asks that we surrender control of everything in our lives. And, that is what it means to be a sacrifice. Jesus paid the ultimate price. The only thing left to place on the altar is . . . me.

I will concede there are times when a disagreement between believers cannot be settled. Despite our most humble efforts, we cannot attain peace with another believer. The command is to go - we are not commanded to settle an argument by sacrificing the basic doctrines of our faith or denying what is true. We do not seek out the other believer to explain our side of the disagreement and convince them we are right in the matter. If needed, we apologize and ask forgiveness. If possible we offer restitution for the wrong we have done.

The one offended is called to remember that he has been forgiven much by God when he first confessed his sins. Forgiveness comes from God the Father, through us, to the other person. This is the basis for restoring damaged relationships as we come to understand how much we have been given by God.

This is a very difficult concept that must handled carefully. I have known Christians who made very effort to mend a relationship, only to sink further into discord. I would suggest that one not make a move in this direction without extended time in prayer and the direction of the Holy spirit. If the other person is unwilling to forgive and settle the dispute, we must practice God's grace toward the other believer and mercy toward ourselves.

When I am troubled over my relationship with another person, I find that I spend more time in prayer, thinking about the changes God needs to make in my life. For the broken relationship that cannot be repaired, Dr. David Stoops suggests that we may need to ask another person to stand in place of the one we have wronged to offer forgiveness and restitution. [3]

In coming to the altar, I must consider whether I have done everything I can to resolve the issue with my brother. When I can honestly answer that all is well with my soul, only then can I fall back on God's mercy and grace. I can release my brother or sister to God's work in their lives without further effort on my part.

There is something powerful in seeing the body of Christ as a corporate body of believers. While confession may begin alone, the sacrament of Communion is to be celebrated together. It is difficult to turn to oneself and offer a wafer, saying, "This is the body of Christ."

An element is missing. The Communion service is corporate, drawing individual believers into one body. We are not called to stand alone. We are called to stand together.

The Lord's Supper is the beginning of what I share with other believers, implemented by our Savior. Yet, we have numerous examples of Christians who drifted away from faith after giving up the fellowship of believers.

I have come to believe that God gave us the time to examine ourselves before participating in Communion in order to repair relationships. This allows the body to function properly without conflict breaking up the community. This can be a radical idea and very difficult for someone who does not handle the effort toward reconciliation well. If you find such an idea difficult, let this settle for a bit.

Jesus understood that the human psyche is vulnerable to temptation and to devising explanations for our sinful behavior. He gave us each other to encourage and to help us stand strong when temptation threatens us. We come together to celebrate the Lord's Supper. Having sought God's forgiveness and worked to resolve differences with others, the sacrament is enough. I know I am sealed under the blood of Christ. When I walk out of the service, I am renewed. In that renewal, I am once again prepared to be part of this community.

We have discussed the elements of communion, how the sacrament began and that it is a corporate practice. We've come to understand that Communion allows us time to mend relationships which underlie the health of the our community of believers.

When we consider what it means to be part of a community, we see that the members of a community have common interests. As Christians it is not enough to acknowledge those common interests alone. We must, in turn, begin to build on those common interests to create a network of believers exalting God and working for common good. To build relationships, we meet together beyond the four walls of our church to encourage and share our lives. A sense of joy and mutual support weave through our relationships until we are truly bound together as family.

Pastor Eugene Peterson explains this by saying, "Christians are a community of people who are visibly together at worship, but who remain in relationship through the week in witness and service." [4]

Building community does not require a new ministry with a director with a list of activities to help us get to know each other. We are already busy with the everyday responsibilities of life. The sense of community should flow out of sharing each others' lives in everyday tasks.

I can think of at least three sets of circumstances where, when successful, this sense of community overflows and enriches all those involved. These circumstances we share in common include the joy and celebration of two individuals joining their lives together in matrimony. Marriage is often followed by the birth of children. We watch and participate in each other's lives as we raise our families.

Then in time, death also becomes a common ground between us. Members may lose a son or daughter, a father or mother. The preparation for an end of life service can be daunting. The members of a community can serve the family of a loved one who has died as well as strengthen their own beliefs as they prepare for challenges later in life.

One of the most difficult times in the life of a church

community is when an individual strays into sin. We are called to bring this individual back into Godly repentence within our community. If we are caught in a cycle of conflict between believers, our ability to work at restoring another may be stunted and the encouragement that flows between two individuals may not happen.

In Ephesians, chapter 4, verse 3, the Apostle Paul calls us to, "Make every effort to keep the unity of the Spirit through the bond of peace." We are called to live in peace yet misunderstandings, prejudice and deliberate betrayal may rend us apart.

Jesus gave us one Lord, one faith and one body of believers. It is man who creates dissension. I am not advocating that we all join the unity movement, suppressing our commitment to the central tenets of our faith. We have vital doctrines that cannot be compromised if we are to remain the body of Christ in this world. If we follow Jesus, the one who gave his life for us, then we will find a way to live together when we agree on those central tenets.

In the next three chapters, we will examine the role of the community within our lives and how we contribute to our local body of believers. First we will look at the celebration of joy. We will next look at how we treat another believer who, being human, has fallen into sin but wishes to reconcile.

Finally, not only does the community serve a role in joy and in restoration but when we are faced with tragedy, we step into the roles of service and offer comfort. Each of these examples will help us explore how the practice of communion draws us closer together as a body of believers.

To a believer casually considering communion, there may seem to be little connection between the sacrament and the spiritual health of a body of believers. Can you imagine trying to celebrate or discipline a church member when the body of believers is torn by strife? God intended communion to resolve our differences so that we can fulfill the role of the church. He compels us to take time to settle differences with other believers before we bring our gifts to him as his altar.

Chapter 5

Celebration: Joy

*"There is a time for everything,
and a season for every activity under heaven:
a time to weep
and a time to laugh,
a time to mourn
and a time to dance."*
Ecclesiastes 3:1, 4

When I think of celebration, the image of David dancing before the Lord comes to mind. Israel witnessed a grown man throwing himself with every ounce of energy into a physical demonstration of love and joy in a celebration of God's goodness.

Like many Christians I was raised in a home where dancing was not one of the approved activities. Today I love dance but my aging body fails to move so generously. I remember the reception following the wedding that brought my daughter and her husband together as man and wife. The music began to rumble out of loudspeakers, washing over the celebrants as a group of young men circled the bride and groom. As the beat echoed against the walls, the men began to jump, straight up, dropping back down to repeatedly rise again. Their laughing faces reflected the joy they took in the celebration for the new husband

and wife.

I have chosen the example of marriage to express joy in part because God used the example of marriage to give us a picture of Christ joining the body of believers to himself. In that union we become one. We are no longer separated from God. What a marvelous reason to celebrate. The idea that we can become one with the omniscient creator is beyond our comprehension.

As we participate in Communion we are about to celebrate this great union between God and the believer. I have first examined myself for sin that remains in my life. I have eaten a small wafer, remembering Christ's body broken for me. Then, the pastor or lay person offers up the wine, saying, "This is my blood shed for you." Points of light sparkle in the dark liquid. Now comes the time to celebrate.

Wine played an important role in celebrating Israel's feasts. Wine was traditionally the symbol of sanctification. Through Jesus' blood are sanctified or made holy before a righteous God. The Jewish celebration of marriage included a cup of wine that was symbolic of the cup of life the two people would share together as they became one. Christians being united as one with Christ and united with each other are themes we understand and celebrate.

Knowing the role of wine within Jewish culture, we further develop our understanding of Jesus' choice of symbols as he called on his disciples to share the wine. He was anticipating a time when through his death and resurrection, the disciples would celebrate their sanctification before God. He was calling on them to celebrate, to give way to joy as their grief over his death receded. The time to mourn had come to an end, the time to celebrate had arrived. [1]

Celebration

We should be known for our love of God, our love of each other and our joy in salvation. I'm wondering if our Communion services have become too somber as we are called to reflect on Christ's death and resurrection. Have we lost the joy the women expressed on the morning of Jesus' resurrection?

How do we show our joy in celebrating our redemption through Christ's blood? Can you imagine a body of believers, jumping up and down in excitement. We are forgiven! We are new creatures! Dancing is definitely one option.

In the early eighteenth century, a religious community known as the Shakers gained notoriety in the national press for their religious expression. They expressed their religious devotion by forming large circles to dance in intricate patterns. People outside of their communities flocked to see their rites. I am not suggesting that we form communal societies that dance in celebration of our salvation but rather that our joy should be so evident to people around us as if we were dancing openly in celebration.

For many churches the joy is restrained. In celebrating God's sacrifice for us, we choose a dignified, reverent response. However, the celebration is not confined to those few moments within the church building but spills out into our lives in the community.

Celebration brings to mind generosity, whether in gifts to each other or an overwhelming desire to be in each other's presence as the staggering realization of what we have been given becomes more evident each day. We want to rejoice with each other as we see God's work in our lives, of God's provision for each of us. I want to see his power in my life more and more evident, revealed in ways that I have never considered. With the Apostle John, I want to celebrate the light that surrounds us. The darkness is gone.

Joy can take many forms. As I celebrate Christ's gift to me, I can turn to my fellow believers, reflecting that joy and celebration toward them.

In the last chapter, we looked at the idea that confession is fundamental to unity and godly relationships between believers when approaching the Lord's Supper. In taking the time to examine ourselves before Communion and to clear up misunderstandings between believers, we are open to God's blessing instead of being distracted by anger toward another believer. Conflict is no longer tearing us apart. Instead, we reflect the love of Christ toward each other.

With this new covenant, our role as believers has evolved and grown. We have become one with Christ and in that unity we have been given privileged responsibility. When my relationship with another believer is clear of misunderstanding or offense, we find a joy in each other's presence. This joy becomes a gift to our Savior as we celebrate and work together.

As we think about our relationship to Christ and to each other, the writer of Hebrews tells us:

> *"Both the one who makes men holy and those who are made holy are of the same family. So Jesus is not ashamed to call them brothers. He says, 'I will declare your name to my brothers; in the presence of the congregation I will sing your praises.'"* Hebrews 2:11-12

In this passage, I find two clues in how I am to celebrate. First, I discover that I have brothers and sisters in Christ. My fellow Christians are more than friends.

They are relatives with a blood bond to me through Jesus. We are not ashamed to claim each other as brother or sister and to declare God's truth to each other. I find that we are on speaking terms!

Secondly, I am to sing God's praises to my family. Some take this literally as they stand together, face to face, melodic notes and words tumbling from their lips. They smile and nod in emphasis at key phrases. Some of them are even on-key!

I have now become an heir of God, a sister to the believers I gather with each Sunday and those in the greater body of Christ. In that role, I am to sing the praises of my Father and his great gift to me. God's praise should tumble from our lips when we are around other believers. As family I should deliberately spend time with my brother and sisters rather than scooting out of the service as quickly as possible for a quick get-away. I cannot speak of God's faithfulness and my joy in salvation he has given me unless I take the time to actually talk with other believers.

I'm not always sure I want to claim the other believers in my church as my brothers and sisters. I am quite certain that they feel the same about me. Yet, because of Jesus, we are family. The Apostle Peter tells us:

"Above all, love each other deeply, because love covers a multitude of sins." [2]

Our love for one another is our calling as Christians. Our love for each other should be evident to all those around us, both in and outside our faith. When we struggle with each other's shortcomings, perseverance and grace toward each other should be born out of our relationship to God, not undermined by our moral failing. The love and grace we receive from God unites with perseverance to maintain the unity with each other. Just as God the Father, God the Son and God the Spirit live in unity, we are called to do the same with each other.

A passage comes to mind out of Psalms 133.

> *"How good and pleasant it is when brothers live together in unity!*
>
> *It is like precious oil poured on the head, running down on the beard, running down on Aaron's beard, down on the collar of his robes.*
>
> *It is as if the dew of Hermon were falling on Mount Zion. For there the Lord bestows his blessing, even life forevermore."* Psalm 133:1-3

Moses and Aaron had their difficult moments! I'm sure Moses could have disappeared into the sand at his feet when he realized that Aaron had taken part in forming the golden calf in the presence of God at the base of Mount Sinai. The last thing Moses wanted to do was face God, knowing how badly his brother had fallen. Yet, when God offered to wipe the Jewish people from the map, Moses pled with God to spare his people, reminding God that the nations were watching. He pled for Aaron's life before an angry God, asking forgiveness for both the nation and his brother. God presents us with their example as brothers living in unity. He reminds us that Moses as God's representative anointed his brother to serve God's people.

While loving each other becomes an integral part of our life as Christians, the Apostle Peter added a new dimension to our relationship with each other.

Celebration

"You are a chosen people, a royal priesthood, a holy nation, a people belonging to God, that you may declare the praises of him who called you out of darkness into his wonderful light. Once you were not a people, but now you are the people of God, once you had not received mercy, but now have received mercy."   I Peter 2:9-10

As priests, we have two responsibilities, one is to lift up praise to our creator and redeemer. The other responsibility is to serve God's people just as the priests served in the tabernacle.

This concept is carried down from the tribal practices of the Old Testament through the Temple's torn curtain into this age of God's grace. God called Moses to anoint his own brother, pouring oil over his head, to signify that he was set apart by God for service. Aaron was to serve God's people as a priest, a mediator between God and his people. With Jesus death, the curtain separating the worshipers from the Holy Place was torn open. We no longer needed a representative before God. We are free to approach him directly. However, the concept of priests serving God and man did not die out but was transformed into a much broader sense. God declared all those who sought his forgiveness to be priests to each other, based on the mercy he had shows us.

As I read the passage in I Peter, I understand that we are all called to a royal priesthood, cast in the role of being a servant to each other. There is a humility in serving each other.

I'm struck by that thought at Communion as I watch the men, sometimes women, serving the bread and the wine. In some denominations they stand at the end of each aisle, passing the elements. In other traditions those serving stand at the front of the sanctuary and administer the wafer and juice to the members who approach the altar. The men are not checking lists to determine whether the supplicant is acceptable to God, based on men's standards. Those passing the plates of wafers, the cups of wine are serving the body just as each of us should have a role in which we serve our brothers and sisters.

I recently heard a story from a Vietnam veteran about a priest who flew into the jungle camp where the soldiers were serving in an active war zone. Bob, the one telling the story, was just a young kid caught up in the draft in the 1960's. Like so many young men who registered for the draft, his number was called and within months, he found himself under live fire in the jungles of Vietnam. Sanitation was crude. Insects and snakes made life difficult for all the men stationed with Bob. They never knew when the enemy would rain live fire down on their camps or catch them in an ambush on patrol.

Bob and his fellow soldiers had been stuck in a jungle camp for months. As they sweated and feared, trying to ignore the discomfort, the loneliness and the desperation, a helicopter descended into the clinging, wet embrace of the vegetation and the ever constant mud. The heavy chop of the blades echoed their heart beats as they stupidly stared at the figure that dropped from the open door. Bob caught a glimpse of a silver cross glinting through the man's fatigues. The chaplain ducked under the blades and ran toward the men as they turned their faces to avoid the airborne grit that penetrated their slitted eyelids.

How long had it been since a chaplain visited their isolated camp? Bob had struggled with loneliness and a sense of abandonment that assaulted the faith he had gained as a young man. The chaplain stood before them, unwrapping his Bible and the sacraments.

As Bob recalls, the chaplain was Catholic. He asked each man who stepped forward about their background of faith. Bob mentioned that he was from a Protestant background. The chaplain knew it would be months more before another chaplain, maybe a Protestant minster, would appear in the clearing. He apologized that the men had not received regular visits from a Protestant chaplain. He almost seemed to apologize for being Catholic.

Turning to Bob, he said, "Though we have different creeds, please allow me to represent God to you today."

Bob tells me he was so glad to have someone, anyone to speak the words of faith to his soul, that he had no issue with their doctrinal differences. He gladly knelt in the mud that day, rejoicing to accept Communion from the hands of a priest. A priest who was intent on serving God. In the ugliness of blood and killing, he willing to pay the cost of mutual sacrifice.

This role of service does not end with the consumption of the bread and wine. The gift of serving each other moves beyond special occasions into our homes to the chores we practice each day. The role of service in humility to each other continues throughout our lives. Serving each other becomes a means of joy, of celebration for all that God has given us.

Our service to each other should be part of our every day routine. I have often longed to join with my sisters over a cup of tea to share our lives and to encourage each other. For the most part, this is something we have lost. If we see someone missing from our fellowship, it should be a clarion call to check on that person to offer support and encouragement. In offering encouragement, we find practical ways to serve, maybe by doing the dishes!

When all is in balance, when we examine ourselves before God, we are free to serve each other without inhibiting the flow of grace. Grace given by God to us, grace in turn given to each other. By restoring damaged relationships before we take Communion we can celebrate freely and joyfully together. This is one of the great gifts of the sacrament of Communion, drawing pardoned sinners together in the presence of God.

Anyone who has tried to dance while balancing a cup of wine and a loaf of bread, comes to know just how awkward service can become. Things gets spilled, awkward moments happen. In our role as priests and brothers, we must allow grace and joy to over-ride our shortcomings, the missed steps. We mop up the spilled wine, counting each moment as a service of joy to our Lord.

If only we could remain in unity and joy. I doubt there is a Christian through the centuries who has not spent at least one moment longing for that family connection when adversity threatened to overwhelm the body of Christ.

Most of us enjoy talking about unity and love in the body. If you're like me, at some point in the discussion, I have this little niggling reminder that due to our humanity, not all remains infinitely peaceful in a body of believers.

What happens when conflict enters the church? How do we resolve the grief that enters the body from the sinful actions of a believer? Along with joy, those times when we confront sin play a role in our understanding of Communion in the Lord's Supper and how God works in our lives.

Chapter 6

Examining the Uncomfortable

Outside the windows of the church, dusk was fading into darkness. The overhead lights, which had once been mere courtesy, were beginning to glow in the dim light, illuminating the white walls of the sanctuary.

We had gathered for the annual conference that brought missionaries from all over the small country to the capital city. They had spent time discussing the plans for the next year, praying for guidance and loving each other's company. There is a common ground among missionaries in countries that are not of their home culture. It is more than missing family or struggling with a strange language. It is the sense that we are pilgrims, longing for a place of our own, yet ready to move on toward a new endeavor. One never quite gets comfortable.

For children, the annual conference was exciting. We gathered in a large group, renewing acquaintance, playing rowdy games and enjoying other children with the same skin color, common language and culture. Just like our parents, we were aliens in a strange land. At the end of the conference, there is a satisfaction, a longing for one's own bed but also a sense of accomplishment in wrapping up another year.

As the final speaker brought his message to a

conclusion, boredom sapped my attentiveness. I watched the edge of light from the setting sun creep up the wall of a home beyond the surrounding courtyard. I marveled at the pink tinge in the sky and longed for one last game of hide 'n seek with so many of us flinging ourselves in desperate pursuit of excellent hiding places.

As the service came to an end, we stood to sing a final song. From the podium, the speaker asked my father to pray, closing the service. Along with those gathered, I waited for him to begin, thinking about the evening ahead.

Silence followed the speaker's request. Dad stuttered a moment, "H...heavenly Father." A deep sigh emanated from him and he fell silent once again. I could feel the tension mounting in the room. People were definitely growing uncomfortable.

"Father God, we come together," Again he tried, falling silent once more.

I stood there, mentally squirming. What was his problem? Everyone must be wondering why he failed to pray. This is what we did, as natural as speaking to each other. Prayer is speaking to God. He broke the silence.

"I'm sorry. I can't pray. Ask someone else."

The tension in the room only rose. The speaker fumbled for a few quick words of his own. When we opened our eyes, despite that strange moment, the missionaries seemed to make every effort to resume life as normal. We left the building, returning to the guest houses near the church where each had spent the last few nights in strange beds.

An hour later I asked my mom, "Why couldn't dad pray tonight?"

"I will tell you," she replied. "I think you are old enough to understand."

That night I learned just how far one can fall. One of the leaders from our mission, a man highly respected and loved by his fellow missionaries, had been unfaithful - to his God, to his wife and to his fellow Christians. As a result the bond of trust was broken. Another result, a child.

With his confession, the other missionaries struggled to deal with the legal ramifications as well as counsel this couple toward forgiveness and reconciliation. My father had respected this man, had looked to him for counsel and enjoyed his friendship. Dad's heart was broken as he considered what had happened. As he struggled to understand and come to resolution, he could not form the words to pray. His heart cried out to God yet his mouth stuttered over each syllable.

We all grieve when another Christian, a beloved member of our Body, chooses to set aside grace and step into sin. We are all sinners. We have all reached for the mercy and grace of our forgiving God. We struggle to live up to a standard that will always be beyond us. Yet when one of us falls, we feel as if we ourselves are injured. In a sense, sin is an injury, a physical break in the Body of Christ. The fellowship that we share within Christ is broken and must be knitted back together.

Unfortunately, this can be a difficult process, exposed to the view of those who do not share our faith. Have you ever heard someone say, "I can't stand to be around Christians. They are just a bunch of hypocrites, saying one thing and doing another."

Ouch! That person would be right. We are not perfect, we are sinners seeking God's grace. And yet, as imperfect individuals we are called together to form one body. The result? Often parts of the body are subject to pain when circumstances set a course different from what God has prescribed for us.

The Body of Christ is community, diverse and yet unified in our core beliefs. We all celebrate the differences we bring to the body. Paul describes the body by individual parts, giving special attention to those members that may be less presentable or harmed in some way.

> *"But God has combined the members of the body and has given greater honor to the parts that lacked it, so that there should be no division in the body, but that its parts should have equal concern for each other. If one part suffers, every part suffers with it; if one part is honored, every part rejoices with it. Now you are the body of Christ and each of you is a part of it."* I Corinthians 12:24a-27

As mortal beings, we find the journey through pain difficult to travel. Anyone who has suffered a serious accident can understand the struggle with physical therapy. When our bodies have returned to health, we know we are not the same as we were before the accident. Whether our scars are fully displayed or hidden in our psyche, we still bear the tenderness of the pain caused by illness or accident.

The same is true with the Body of Christ. We fall, we get hurt. We hurt others in the process because we are all part of the same body, as Paul notes in the passage above. The whole body feels the pain of even the smallest injury. We cannot leave that injured member behind, refusing to acknowledge the existence of pain. If a member found in sin will confess and seek forgiveness, we are to forgive ad strive to restore him to fellowship. Just as with an injury to the physical body, we may be involved in months of counseling, akin to physical therapy, trying to restore the wounded part. Before we even begin to work with a damaged member, we need to ensure that we have repaired our own relationships so that grace may flow freely.

In this story I've told, one man committed a sin yet it wounded all the missionaries that gathered at the annual conference. They did not participate in that sin and yet they suffered the pain that descended on the body of believers in that country. Not only were these missionaries drawn together, serving under a common Mission Board, they were gathered in the only English-speaking church in the country. They did not have the option of leaving that body to attend another church down the street. This man was one of their own and they bore a responsibility for him. There had been a break in the common communion, an injury to the local body of believers.

A committee was assigned to make decisions regarding discipline and how to move forward. One of their tasks was to determine how to restore their brother. The first step was taken when this man confessed to the sin that he had committed. Both man and wife confessed to shortcomings in their marriage. They took financial responsibility for the child that was born. After returning to the United States, this couple submitted to Christian counseling. While they did not return to the mission field, their marriage was restored and they began serving in their local church again.

In that process, the members of the body, served this couple, helping to restore their relationship with each other and with God. As I discussed in the previous chapter, this is what a priest does, bringing God's truth and love to hurting people. We do not live out our lives alone, speaking only to God. Communion means that we weave our lives into a common tapestry.

I am wounded when people complain about all those hypocrites in the church and swear that they will never darken the door of a church again because of the problems within a church. Thinking of Paul's analogy, they have just self amputated themselves from the body and are trying to go it alone. Or possibly, they join another church and believe that all will be well, even though they did not work to heal the injury before they left the first congregation.

When we leave the body under difficult circumstances without first mending the wounds that have been inflicted, the injury begins to fester. We are unable to completely support and bless each other as God intended. Jesus gave us the Lord's Supper to remind us to mend our differences and to serve as a catalyst toward reconciliation. Once again, consider:

> *"Therefore, if you are offering your gift at the altar and there remember that your brother has some thing against you, leave your gift there in front of the altar. First go and be reconciled to your brother; then come and offer your gift."* Matthew 5:23

Just as sin inflicts injury to the body, so confession and repentance restore fellowship between believers. Ultimately, we all fall short, whether the sin is publically displayed or hidden from sight for a time. We cannot accuse others of behaving hypocritically when we are all sinners before God. This is not what Jesus intended when he first chose his disciples and began to build his church. There is a better way. Let me tell you a story about David, the battle-hardened leader who would become king of Israel.

Not days, not weeks! These men had lived in the desert for years. The struggle to survive in a harsh desert sapped the fluids from their bodies, left them scarred, desperate for home and family. They longed to return to their homes and resume a life free of conflict. But the king sitting on the throne of Israel, the anointed of God, sought their lives. He sought one life in particular. Saul hated David. He wanted him dead as only a madman can dream. Each of David's men had fled from their homes, wandering into his camp, one by one, some days two or three. They came to David and learned to live in the wilderness as the desert offered refuge from a madman.

By contrast, David was a leader, gifted by God. He grew with the challenge as the number of men in his camp rose toward 600. Together they found the water holes, scavenged for food and sought security from Saul's spies. But the day came, when this life was beyond what they could endure. They sought refuge with Israel's enemies, the Philistines of Gath.

Achish, the ruler of Gath, was no fool. He knew of David. He had heard of Saul's hatred for David and saw an opportunity. In giving David and his men shelter from Saul and homes for their families, he gained a force of mercenaries to fight his enemies in Israel. I've wondered how he thought David could fight against his own kinsman. Achish must have believed that in time David would become so hated in Israel that he would have no choice but to loyally serve the Philistines.

David had been a canny survivalist for too long to fall for such a scheme. Frequently, he set out from Gath on raids into the neighboring territories. Returning to Gath, Achish would arrogantly survey the plunder of the raids and inquire where David had last fought his enemies. David would reply that he had raided the tribes of Israel that lived along the Negev desert.

Achish must have been unaware of the history of the descendants of Caleb living along the Negev. Caleb had been one of the first spies when Israel arrived on the banks of the Jordan a century earlier. When faced with Israel's fear, Caleb had forcefully called Israel to take the land for their birthright, unafraid of the tribes that inhabited the land between the Jordan and the shores of the Mediterranean. Forty years later, when Israel returned from wandering the desert to enter Canaan, Caleb claimed a section of the mountainous south and the Negev desert as his to conquer, his to inherit. His descendants were no less valiant, living on the edge of the wilderness.

David had been raiding and stealing from neighboring tribes, not Israel and the descendants of Caleb, but those in liaison with the Philistines of Gath. He left no witnesses and brought back plunder that would satiate the curiosity of Achish.

As David lived in Gath, the Philistines commanders began to plot against Israel, drawing up battle plans. Saul, the king of Israel plotted his own moves against Israel's enemies, camping strategically in Jezreel where he might launch a campaign against the Philistines. As the Philistines assembled for battle, David and his 600 men marched at the tail end of the Philistine battle column. In alarm, the Philistine commanders turned to Achish and demanded to know what he was thinking. When they came to battle with Israel, David could turn on the rear flank of the Philistine forces and catch them in a pincher movement. Saul at the front, David to the rear. What chance did they stand? What better way for David to be restored to the good graces of a mad king, they asked.

Despite Achish's reassurances, his commanders demanded that David return to Gath. I see God's provision in that demand. For years, God had provided for the needs of David and his men. Now once again, he was providing an escape from the inevitability of facing their own countrymen in battle.

They returned to Gath, the journey taking three days. As they followed the narrow paths, the men began to search the horizon, noting landmarks along the route that assured them they were drawing near to a reunion with their families. Then one man cried loudly, pointing to a faint smudge on the horizon. Smoke, the telltale sign of a town burned to the ground. Rushing over the rough ground, they found the town burned by their enemies, the Amalekites, one of the tribes that they had raided. Suddenly they didn't feel so invincible, so smug about their duplicity toward Achish.

Their families had disappeared and the tracks left at the edge of the town gave no doubt regarding their fate. They were captive, part of the plunder of this raid.

Worn from the fever of battle, their anguish over this loss turned them against the one who had first led them to Gath. They looked to the leader who had called on them to follow the battle columns of the Philistines, away from their families in the face of the raiders. David! Caught by anguish over the loss of their families, they turned to run their knives across David's throat, to tear his limbs from his torso.

Eugene Peterson in his book on the Psalms paints a picture of David that resonates for leaders in Christian practice. 1 Here was a man who had struggled to lead those who sought him out in the desert. He had not called them to give up their homes, to join his band of desperate men.

He accepted the challenge of men who sought a leader. He struggled to mold them into a force who followed the true God, who worshiped Jehovah. He had lived with them in deprivation, eating the poor food, sleeping on the ground, cold, desperate. He had not sought to place himself above them. He had struggled to build a body of believers in the wilderness. Yet now, when the enemies of Israel had attacked, they turned on him. Did David think this was unfair? 2

I am struck by David's response. He didn't draw his sword and offer to take on any ingrate. He didn't run in despair from the howling mob. He threw himself before the Lord, the God of heaven and earth. He sought God's guidance. And, God stood by him.

Yes, they rescued their families. More importantly, both David and his men learned another lesson in relying on God. David made sure that Israel knew of God's provision for his men in that he sent portions of the bounty that he took from the Amalekites to the neighboring towns. The story is found in I Samuel 30:1-26.

When we cry out against other believers, when we despise someone who has fallen into sin, what have we done? We have disregarded the grace given to us by God. We have broken the communion that belongs between brothers. We belong to the howling mob rather than being the one who seeks God's guidance.

When the man found in adultery confessed his sin to fellow Christians, they could have disavowed any further relationship with him. Instead, they came to stand with him, guiding, advising, bringing him into repentance and forgiveness. They didn't leave the wounded behind. Such grace is beyond human capacity. This was God's transforming power in the body of Christ.

Apart from God's spirit, this sense of Godly community is not easy to achieve. There are several deterrents that seem to work against us. As I was considering the subject of community, I stumbled across some comments by secular author Philip Slater. He argues that we all conduct a search for privacy, a respite from the crowds, from the public image we must maintain when we are around other people. He further suggests that our irritability with each other grows out of that search for privacy when we emerge from our self-prescribed cocoons. We are jarred by the traffic, the crowds, the requirement to respond in a socially acceptable means to this assault on our senses.

This search for privacy is the complete opposite of what we are trying to achieve within the body of Christ. God did not send us out into the world alone. He gave us the body of believers to support, to encourage, to come alongside, building each other up when life is tough.

One deterrent to building a Godly community might lie in how we talk to each other when we meet at church. We all tend to gravitate toward small talk. We prefer to place people into convenient boxes that can be stored away without requiring an emotional investment from us. It is easier to simply identify another person by the job he performs or a task that is required rather than knowing him as flesh and blood, a person with real needs, who bleeds when cut.

When we come to intimately know another person, we are confronted by his humanity. We find out what hurts him, where he is awkward or less than comfortable. Our polite exterior may start to slip. And then what? This is community. Knowing each other intimately without being torn limb from limb by adversity sets Christians apart from the world. We step out of our insulated cocoons and allow life to get messy.

When we consider getting to know each other, we have a second deterrent in fear. What if we cannot find a solution to any rift that might occur. Today, we tend to cast off the responsibility for resolving differences by saying, 'We agree to disagree.' As often as this statement is used, I am not sure that it is helpful in mending our relationships. God's grace may require that we do more than agree to disagree. I have found that if I cannot stand to be in the presence of another person with whom I disagree, a person with whom I have patched up a relationship, then there is more work to do in mending the relationship. That effort begins with prayer, seeking God's direction in my actions toward the other
person.

The sacrament of Communion is not performed alone just as the communion of being part of the body of Christ is not lived without other believers. I've met people who prefer to worship God alone without the distraction of being around other Christians. They decry the hypocrites, the strife among other believers as just grounds to stay away from established groups of Christians.

As we examine this sacrament of our faith, given by Jesus before his death, we discover that the sacrament is practiced corporately. As we think about Communion, we realize the relationships we have with other people, the same people we celebrate with, may be keeping us from a genuine love of God and the body of Christ. The command to examine oneself, and in turn to act on that examination, takes on a vitality as we act on our confession before God.

If we fail to seek forgiveness when we sin, there can

be deadly consequences. We have an enemy that seeks to destroy us. He will not fail to use anger and hurt as a weapon to attack the individual and the body of Christ. Without confession and forgiveness, anger will fester like a sore that will not heal. Sin divides and separates us from God and from each other.

> *"Therefore, whoever eats the bread or drinks the cup of the Lord in an unworthy manner will be guilty of sinning against the body and blood of the Lord. A man ought to examine himself before he eats of the bread and drinks of the cup. For anyone who eats and drinks without recognizing the body of the Lord, eats and drinks judgement on himself. That is why many among you are weak and sick, and a number of you have fallen asleep. But if we judged ourselves, we would not come under judgement. When we are judged by the Lord, we are being disciplined so that we will not be condemned with the world."* I Corinthians 11:27-32

This passage gives us a course of action. As we recognize our sins, we examine ourselves, seeking God's forgiveness and grace. Then, in turn we extend the same forgiveness and grace to others in the body. We receive a gift beyond all measure which we extend to others. In a sense, we have come the full circle back to God's covenant with us. We can follow his commands and be blessed or we can fail to work though the difficulties and fall under judgement.

As with David's story, the relationships within the body of the Christ can be our biggest sense of sorrow. How can my Christian brother, my sister, be so insensitive to the grief they have caused?

By the same measure God has granted us, we must be willing to forgive others when they ask for our forgiveness. This can be a gift to both the one who gives and the one who receives as mercy and grace overflow. Whether asking or giving forgiveness, we cannot fail to mend relationships.

David understood grace in a way that makes us look like anaemic novices. When a band of howling warriors stood ready to sacrifice him to their grief, he turned to God. He brought his men with him into the presence of the Holy one.

Like David, when faced with estrangement from other members of the body, we can live the example of a man who understands his position before God. When division comes, we can fall on our faces before God and worship him. As we acknowledge our own failings and worship the almighty God, the hypocrites don't seem to be so important. In our response to God, we can bring others to see his work in our lives.

The sacrament of Communion draws us into repentance and restoration with each other. To make this personal, I've come to realize that I cannot participate in repentance and restoration apart from others. If I reject the body of Christ as represented by the church, I am depriving myself of God's work in my life. With this renewed perspective, I find myself creeping back to the church, to the body of believers and burrowing back into fellowship. I eagerly seek God's work in my life through his church.

When we face dissension within the body of believers, when sin strikes at the core of our assembly, we must first turn to God and seek his guidance. In turn, we are given the opportunity, by God, to share once more the sorrow and joy that he experiences in dealing with us. The fellowship with other believers becomes one of God's great gifts to us.

> *"Who is a God like you, who pardons sin and forgives the transgression of the remnant of his inheritance. You do not stay angry forever but delight to show mercy. You will again have compassion on us; you will tread our sins underfoot and hurl all our iniquities into the depths of the sea."* Micah 7:18-19

Chapter 7

Flesh to the Scaffold

> *"Dear friends, do not be surprised at the painful trial you are suffering, as though something strange were happening to you. But rejoice that you participate in the sufferings of Christ, so that you may be overjoyed when his glory is revealed."*   I Peter 4:12-13

What is the worst thing you can imagine happening to you? The very worst that life can throw at you. Illness, the loss of bodily function, financial bankruptcy. All of these would be difficult to handle. One of those moments came for us when our son was killed at age 22 on April 20, 2005.

That afternoon, two Marines crossed the porch. We met them at the door, already knowing the reality of their announcement. Before they could speak a word we were struggling to come to grips with what they had to say. In that moment, I reached out and once again grabbed onto my faith with both hands.

We think of faith as something that is part of us but in a moment of upheaval, it may be something that we have to consciously incorporate into our thinking until we can regain a sense of balance. After the two officers left, my husband and I sat for a few minutes trying to come to terms with the news and what we must do that evening.

We had to tell our daughters and family. Friends would want to know and we must talk to our pastor to begin preparation for the funeral.

Later that evening, two of our pastors, one of their wives and another woman arrived unannounced to pray, to listen, to simply be there. By the next day, the phone began to ring, visitors came by unannounced. We live in a relatively small community and the news spread through word of mouth, by radio and newspaper. Through us, the war in Iraq suddenly became personal for many people in our town. We were overwhelmed by the response we received. In that response, our body of believers played an important role.

As Sunday approached we considered whether to attend church, knowing we would be inundated by questions. We knew our local body was the place we both needed to be, the place we met with other members of Christ's body on a weekly basis. Yet, I felt a sense of dread about appearing publicly. We were exhausted from interacting with people. The members of our church would have understood if we had chosen not to show up that Sunday but the worship service was where we needed to be, the place we met with God, corporately.

We slipped in after the service had started. I felt as if a sense of awareness passed through the rows of seats. Unspoken, the word spread that we had joined the assembly. The hymns, the choruses rose around us as we took our seats. As we listened, the selection of music began to sink in.

"You are my hiding place. You always fill my heart with songs of deliverance whenever I am afraid. I will trust in you." This was followed by "I cast all my cares upon you. I lay all of my burdens down at your feet. And anytime

I don't know what to do, I will cast all my cares upon you."

The words of familiar songs slowly penetrated the fuzz in our brains and I began to look at the congregation for the first time. They weren't staring at us as they followed the worship team but they knew we were there. The musicians had chosen songs that dealt with loss and turning to God for comfort. Some of the people across the room were quietly wiping tears away. The mood was somber.

I slowly began to realize that these people were grieving with us. They felt a sense of loss. Some of them had watched Marty grow up, racing through the very rows of chairs we occupied. We were not alone in grieving our son. The congregation had closed ranks and grieved with us. In that moment I once again recognized the value of the gift given to body of Christ.

Why bring up such a personal loss when discussing the Lord's Supper? As Jesus met with his disciples that last evening before he was arrested, he asked them to share his suffering. In turn, we are called to share in the suffering of Christ. At this moment, in Western culture, we will not hang on a cross or endure severe beatings. Instead we experience that suffering through our lives on earth as part of the community called by the name, Christian. When one member is hurt, the rest of the body should share in that pain to some degree. We are not present to stare and whisper but to stand with the one who has stumbled, who is in pain. As Paul wrote in his letter to the church in Galatia.

> *"Share each other's troubles and problems, and so obey our Lord's command."* Galatians 6:2 LB

After the service, a young man approached us, wearing a jacket in the familiar camouflage pattern. He was a member of the local National Guard unit and frequently wore the jacket for warmth.

"How could you wear military camouflage today?" I asked.

He responded, "I didn't think you would be here today."

"Where did you think I would be?" I replied. "This is my home, this is where I belong. I needed to be here." I hugged him for I realized in that moment he also was struggling with the sufficiency of God's grace.

The body of Christ. Does it mean more than a phrase we casually repeat as a way of referring to the church? Does it have a reality in our lives? I have often railed against my local body for their lack of concern, for their petty conflicts, for not being what I thought was required of them. At other times, a warm glow has spread through me when unity seemed to click in place.

When our lives were transformed by tragedy, the body of Christ stood with us, exactly as presented in the scriptures. Their love shone through the darkness of grief. They prayed for us, fed us and encouraged us.

That Monday, I realized that the funeral was not just for our members. The community was coming and the church was not large enough to handle the crowd. We resisted the suggestion to move the funeral to communal facilities. Our church, a building of stone and wood, has stood before the people of our town as a statement of faith for those who worship inside it's doors. This church building was a part of the faith we chose to demonstrate publicly.

I called the church office and explained the situation, asking if an audio feed might be routed into a reception room near the auditorium. The secretary assured me that the men had been working on just such an idea that morning. Again, I was overwhelmed to know the body of Christ was reaching out, anticipating our needs and responding without being asked to help.

Our local body of believers, including some from other churches, stepped forward to usher visitors to their seats, to work the sound board, to lead the music. This body of believers knew the community was watching and in their efforts, they outdid themselves in representing Jesus Christ. When the funeral service began, many of the members chose to sit in the fellowship hall so that the people from outside the church could find seats in the sanctuary. If we had been torn by division, these men and women would have struggled to work together. Instead, God's grace was on display to those who attended the service.

Each day as we emptied our mail box we received cards assuring us of the support of the body of believers surrounding us. There were some who called, broken over the loss, unable to adequately express their sorrow for us. We spoke with them about our faith and in turn were built up by those who shared that belief in a sovereign God. One of the most rewarding responses came from a man outside the church. He attended the funeral and later marveled to one of our members, "I couldn't believe how good I felt after that funeral. No one was angry, no one was blaming anyone. They really seemed to focus on God."

With our son's death, we were able to speak with a large number of people about the God we worship and his sufficiency to meet our deep sadness. We were able to show others that we trusted our God in all things. In turn, our small community of believers demonstrated their care for us as the town watched.

As we partake of Communion, we sip our wine, chew and swallow the bread as members of the body of Christ. Those physical elements may quickly disappear from our conscious thought when they are the opening gambit in the great communion in Christ. We are called to so much more. We are called to sorrow, to share in the suffering of Christ.

This can be a bit jolting when actually confronted by sorrow in our everyday lives. Yet, suffering with others is part of sharing in the suffering and, conversely, in the joy of Christ. We set aside our own self-absorption and begin to see others as Jesus sees them. Communion represents the threshold we cross when we accept our responsibility to each other. The command to examine ourselves during the Communion service causes us to look in three directions: First we look at God, then we examine ourselves. Finally, our gaze extends to others. We share in the sorrow of Christ by our participation in life of the body. God uses our participation in the body of Christ and the world around us to bring comfort to a hurting world. In return, this brings us into deeper communion with him.

When we take the bread and the wine, we have begun to participate in a larger calling than our daily lives might offer us. We share God's sorrow over mankind. How we handle sorrow and suffering says much about our understanding of God and how he relates to us. God is glorified in the compassion shown toward suffering and sorrow in others.

Several months after we lost Marty, I heard of another family who figuratively lost a child. The child had not died. At nine years of age, she had been molested by a family member. Her mother, for the safety of the child, sent her away and the little girl was willing to go. She was sent to live with the non-custodial parent for her own safety. The child was torn between loyalty to her mother and the grief caused by the abuser. They have spoken only once in two years.

If I were that mom, I would find it so easy to get angry and feel as if I were treated unfairly in the situation. What right did that family member have to molest the little girl and deprive her of the love of her mom? But that was not the end of the pain.

Unlike our experience in losing our son, the mother did not gain the support of her local congregation. She felt that in order to protect her child, she must keep the details of what had happened away from public consumption. She did not tell the church body as a whole. The couple left the congregation for over a year as they struggled to live without her daughter. Unfortunately, the members of our congregation did not note the couple's absence and failed to follow up. This couple did not receive the love and support of the body of Christ at a critical time. I do suspect that during this difficult time, they came to understand the sorrow that God often feels for us in our failures.

Our local body of believers may fail to respond when we come through a difficult time but the omniscient God never fails to be present when we struggle. He has promised upon his Word He will always be with us.

First he sends his Spirit, the comforter, to be present with us when we are caught in deep sorrow. Then, he works through the body of Christ to achieve his perfection in our lives. This is the underlying reality of the church. We gather to support and love each other as an expression of our love for God. When necessary, we counsel and we grieve. Keeping our relationships well repaired is critical in this bond. The common communion is not something we can casually release from our lives without consequence.

A we come to a summation of a discussion on commion, I've thought about what would happen if commnion were forcibly removed from our churches. What if I were denied communion for some preceved fault? Would we so casually dismiss the call to participate if we were forbidden the Sacrament? In the next chapter let's consider the security of God's promise held in the Lord's Supper.

Chapter 8

Melting Hearts

It seems so obvious that little sins beget bigger sins and they in turn beget bigger ones yet. If such sins are not taken care of quickly, there will be consequences one would just as well not have to resolve. I wonder why we don't learn that lesson early on. Indeed, we do learn it and then immediately forget until the next time.

We've looked at how the community functions in three different circumstances that arise in a church. I would note that a group of believers might find it difficult enough to celebrate, to mend and to grieve on any ordinary day. But imagine if a community is torn by strife. How do we function when members are in conflict with each other. The idea that we mend our rifts with other members before we attend to the Lord's Supper assumes a new vitality as we consider how we serve each other in community.

In this new life, we see joy and celebration as we consider what God has given each of us in his love, in his forgiveness and in serving each other. We see restoration when a person falls to sin and openly repents. We seek to comfort the damaged sinner even as we walk beside them to strengthen and guide back to our Father. We seek to comfort those who are struggling with loss. We do this out of love for our Savior, rather than some sense of duty.

In discussing how the body of Christ is to function within a community, I do not want to suggest that this is easy to accomplish.

Sin yet remains to trouble our lives and tempt us, shredding relationships we never meant to damage. We are human with a nature born in sin, redeemed only by Jesus' blood. I frequently struggle with my own body of believers, wishing others cared more for fellow congregants. I find that my feelings get hurt and the one who hurt me sees no need to apologize. In that moment, how tempting it would be to walk away from that community of believers.

When I work in the kitchen, I find that my blades grow dull and I turn to the knife cabinct where I keep a sharpening stone. As I draw the blade of a dull knife repeatedly across the stone at a forth-five degree angle, the edge of the blade is sharpened by the friction with the stone. To gain that sharpened edge, I must remove microscopic particles of steel from the dull edge through friction.

Human beings are not made of metal. Our fragile personalities are easily damaged when a rough attitude, an unkind word collides with our tender feelings. I may never have intended to damage another but suddenly find an interaction with another person exploding into fireworks. I turn, I draw back, seeking to avoid a ration of pain to my own fragile personality.

At times, I have even claimed my actions were intended to sharpen another person as iron sharpens iron. More like the dull edge of my knife has only wounded another believer. Who was I to speak for God? In turn, I've felt the sharp edge of criticism from others and wondered if they spoke the truth I needed to hear.

Was this what God intended when he designed the church? Does he need us to drag out the sharpening stone when he is fully capable of melting our iron hearts in his forge? Iron begins to melt at 2,800 degrees Fahrenheit. God, in his timing, melts our cold hearts in the warmth of his discipline. He does not need us to do the work of the forge for him. He will use us without our first stepping forward to volunteer our service.

Jon once had a family.* Now they were estranged, broken. Each had moved in a different direction. The church they had once attended together was torn by strife, with charges of poor leadership and undue influence over the members of the fellowship. Jon was frightened over that influence in the lives of his family. The grief, the anger that lingered after the split was understandable. No one wants their family torn away from them.

As we talked about that struggle, Jon began to tell me a story about an evening in that church. On this particular evening communion was served as part of the larger agenda. In the months prior to this evening he was describing, he had observed the slow slide toward a church community based on the leadership of one man, rather than the leadership of Jesus Christ. Slowly the members of the body drifted away from the guidance of scripture to rely more on the decisions of this man. In turn, this individual wrapped their lives ever tighter in his grip.

Jon questioned what was happening, constantly pointing to the inerrancy of scripture and insisting that the church must maintain the sovereignty of Christ in all teaching. For his efforts, he came under a cloud of suspicion. He was accused of a rebellious attitude and of disobedience to the leadership. His faith, and his conversion, were questioned. In response to the accusations, he repeatedly

---

Name changed to protect Jon & his family.

assured the doubters that his faith remained strong in Jesus Christ and that he only wanted the same for the body of believers.

Yet, he could feel a crisis coming. He feared that in time the leadership would demand complete capitulation or he would be removed from the fellowship. His wife and children remained under the sway of the leadership. He feared he was losing his family. He fought for them, he fought for the integrity of his own faith.

But I want him to tell this story:

"Things had been getting bad for some time. I continued to question the teaching that was being given in the meetings. I sensed a confrontation was coming.

This particular weekend, we had a retreat for just the men. A lot of confrontation was going on, the men being challenged in their commitment to the leadership. I hadn't said much but everyone knew where I stood. The teaching had been leading toward the idea that only those who were in agreement with the teachings of this particular church were eligible to take Communion. You know the reference in I Corinthians about examining yourself before you take Communion. We were told that if we disagreed with the teaching, we were not in good standing with our brothers. We should not take Communion.

That final evening, we gathered. The retreat had been very emotional, very difficult up to that point. I was having a tough time. I reached out as the plates went by and took a portion. There was this young man who was part of the group and he came up to me as I took the bread and the juice. He asked if I could step outside for a moment.

I was afraid. This man was a body builder. He was big. Not just big from working out. He was tall. He had a big frame. He was intimidating. And I knew that if he objected to my taking communion, he could hurt me.

As we stepped out of the room he asked me, "Jon, are you going to take Communion."

I looked at him and in that moment, I was overwhelmed with all the conflict that had evolved over those last few months. I held out the elements of Communion, my hands shaking.

"This is between me and God," I told him forcefully. "And no one, not even you, can come between me and God. There is nothing you can do to sever that relationship between me and God!"

The young man stared at me for a moment and then said, "OK, OK, I was just wondering what you were going to do."

As Jon told me the story, he cupped his hands out in front of his face, as if he were still gripping two small items. His hands shook with the force of his emotion. It had been years since the incident, yet he still felt passionately about that moment when his right to take Communion had been challenged, leaving him feeling as if his faith were under attack.

I've thought about the implications of that difficult time since he told me the story. No one has ever tried to separate me from the practice of my faith. No one has stepped forward to forbid me Communion based on my perceived walk with my God.

We are called to examine ourselves before communion. We are not called to examine our neighbor. Ultimately, God is our judge, the one who will decide if we practiced our faith judiciously.

God pursues a relationship with us but it is man who

attempts to place limitations on that covenant, to decide what can be done and what would be deemed as separating us from God. Man usurps God's authority. This is an important point. When we earnestly seek God, no one can forbid us to approach God. We expect challenges from outside the church but to face confrontation within the body often comes very unexpectedly. Yet, when we take God's word in hand and compare our lives to the words written by the Apostle Paul, we have all we need to stand in righteousness before God.

This is at the basis of the covenant between God and me. Or between God and you. While Communion may be given corporately, the covenant between God and each of us remains an individual agreement. For a third party to step into the agreement is kin to a legal challenge. Such a challenge might happen in human courts but we are dealing with the God of Universe. He says,

> *"Who will bring any charge against those whom God has chosen. It is God who justifies. Who is he that condemns?. Christ Jesus who died - more than that, who was raised to life - is at the right hand of God and is also interceding for us. Who shall separate us from the love of Christ. Shall trouble or hardship or persecution or famine or nakedness or danger or sword. "* Romans 8:33-35

and further in verse 38:

> *"For I am convinced that neither death nor life, neither angels nor demons, neither the present nor the future, nor any powers, neither height nor depth, nor anything else in all creation, will be able*

to separate us from the love of God that is in Christ Jesus our Lord." Romans 8:38-39

For me, those verses say it all. There is nothing that can come between God and me. Communion is the representation of that covenant. We take the bread and the wine in remembrance of his sacrifice for each one of us. When Jesus died, he reconciled the old issues between God and man. We are now justified through his righteousness, settled on us before God the father.

On the day that all in heaven and earth stood still to witness the death of the son of God, the curtain in the Jewish temple was torn. No longer were we kept from God by a physical limitation. We can approach the Creator of the Universe, the one who gave all to save us from condemnation. We are now in Communion with him. No one can come between us and God.

When man attempts to place his limitations on us, attempts to point out our record of sin and failure, we turn and make the case. We claim what has been rightfully awarded to us. We plead the ancient script of a covenant written in blood.

This is not to say that if we know that another member is flagrantly sinning before the members of a church and the secular community, we cannot intervene. In writing to the Corinthian church, Paul noted that the sacrament was being dishonored by the actions of some members. He decried the presence of sin being tolerated within that body of believers. With a clarion call he demanded that the sin be confronted and either repentence take place or those members who refused to confess and repent be ejected from the church.

Does this sound like a similar challenge such as Jon faced? After all, members of that body were questioning whether he was defiant in the face of their concern. In any case of church discipline, should we not allow God to convict the sinner and hope that given time, that person would repent?

I would note that Jon was not questioning God's leadership in his life but rather the demand for unquestioning submission to a man.

In the sacrament that Jesus initiated, we come to understand that this practice is to be celebrated together, not individually. When you or I confess our sin at the foot of the cross, we receive God's forgiveness and are brought into the body of Christ as one forgiven for all time. In this, no one can forbid us from sharing in this sacrament once we have examined ourselves before God and asked his forgiveness.

Finally as believers, we are called to live with each other in Christ. We may wish to alter these beliefs and this calling to make our lives more comfortable. Ultimately, in obedience to Christ we always return to the foot of the cross. We are reminded that at the cross we find forgiveness, we find celebration.

Once again, consider a definition of Communion: *The bearing with each other in daily life is the living of our faith in each other's presence.*

Communion brings the actual act of grace into our lives. I would argue that through the act of reconciliation with our brothers, we do indeed experience God's grace.

As I researched the practice of Communion within the different denominations. I found that we too easily give up the practice of Communion and sharing the Lord's Supper together. As such we are in danger of losing something vital in our churches. We have surrendered our birthright. As noted, a church I previously attended in the jungles of Ecuador sees no need to practice Communion. In urban America, some denominations celebrate Communion once a quarter. In my church, we celebrated the Lord's Supper every other Sunday through some complain that this is too often.

There could come a day when Christians are persecuted in every nation throughout the world. The countries under the influence of communism and Islam already persecute Christian believers. For Christians to gather as one, draws the attention of authorities, bringing arrest and torture.

A columnist in World Magazine recalls visiting a non-sanctioned church that met in an open air market in China. The small gathering was concealed by market stalls and tapestries and verbal expression of faith was expressed very cautiously. One never knew who might be listening on the other side of a thin wall of fabric. As they brought the service to a close the leader selected the closing hymn. The columnist describes how she began to sing, suddenly realizing her voice was the only audible sound in the small gathering. In the open air market, the hymns are sung by silently mouthing the words, no sound to draw attention.

Jesus was there, among his believers. No human authority could keep those believers from their faith in the one of who had purchased their souls.

Thinking of this columnist's story leads me to the final story of this book, to a young woman who went to China.

Chapter 9

As One

A special grace is required to set aside plans in the prime of life and teach English for two years far from home. A special grace is required to withstand the lack of comfort while missing family and the comfort we take for granted. But then, Lynn believed God was calling her to China as an English teacher.

She was accepted by a non-profit organization and assigned to a province in western China. We have changed both her name and left out the name of the organization to protect their efforts as Christians in a communist country. Christianity is not well-received by the government censors who espouse the party line when confronted by a belief that is contrary to the teachings of communism. When Lynn and her colleagues first set foot in China, they were invited to a welcome banquet. After greeting them, the speaker announced that he understood that many of them held beliefs that were not to be promoted during their time in China. He did not deny them the right to believe as they chose as guests of the government of China. They were simply to keep their beliefs to themselves. Lynn took a sudden interest in the decor, unwilling to betray through even her facial expression her purpose in coming to China under the scrutinizing gaze of government censors. She was fully qualified to teach English as this had been part of her studies for both her bachelor and master's degrees. But her real purpose in coming to China had been to share her faith in a very dark country.

She was assigned to teach English at a university with about 20,000 students, including graduate level scholars. Unlike the American campuses, most of the students lived on campus in a forest of high rise dorms. She recalls that the buildings were seldom more than eight floors as any building nine floors or more required an elevator. On average eight students lived in each room with bunk beds lining the walls and a small cabinet for possessions. To gain some privacy, they would hang skimpy curtains around their bunks.

Her apartment, along with those of other teachers, was on the far end of the campus from the student housing. She accessed the apartment building by passing through an enclosed walkway from an academic building. The interior walls of the buildings were often covered with ice during the winter, leaving the students and faculty shivering as they struggled to process the lessons. During the warmer months, students and faculty traded icy temperatures for sweltering
conditions.

Lynn recalls that the students' lives were filled with stress. With China's one child policy, the pressure to succeed was overwhelming. Tie that to the crowded conditions in the dormitories and it was not uncommon for the symptoms of stress to be a part of the everyday struggle to live.

Lynn was a curiosity to her students whom she eagerly invited to her home. First, there were her clothes. She changed them, every day. It was not uncommon for the students to wear the same clothes for a week at a time.

The fact that she changed her outfit daily, even though she simply rotated three outfits throughout the week left her students convinced that she must be a wealthy American. And then there were the walls of her apartment. She painted them in bright colors. This was unheard of in a society upon which communism had inflicted uniformity. The students never grew tired of discussing her painted walls, uncertain of how to describe their own reaction toward the colors. This in turn was entertaining to Lynn.

Inviting the students to her apartment, gave her the opportunity, she hoped, to develop relationships that would allow her to share her faith in Jesus Christ. She was not alone in this pursuit as the sponsoring organization had assigned two other teachers to the same campus. Other organizations, including the Peace Corps, had also sent teachers. But there was a difference between the teachers of this non-profit organization and the teachers from the Peace Corps. Those differences, over time, became sharply defined. During their off hours, the culture shock was driven deep into each of the foreigners. Most of them spent time watching American TV programs and discussing the episodes with other teachers. Lynn longed to spend time with her students and began to schedule less time with her countrymen. It was not uncommon for the teachers to go out to local bars during the evenings, and this was contrary to the values that Lynn had set for herself as a Christian.

She struggled to understand the other Christian teachers as well. At times, two of the women seemed cynical and sarcastic in their reactions to their Chinese students. All three had come to China for the purpose of sharing their faith. These attitudes did not seem conducive toward that goal. Lynn found herself questioning their methods and motivation. And yet, when they met for prayer together, she marveled as these two women poured out their hearts to the Lord for their students. The cynicism and the outpouring seemed at odds. She felt as if everyday she lived on the edge of the kingdom of God, witness to the struggle between the forces of Satan and the angels of God.

The Christian teachers met each Sunday for worship when classes were in session. Between the three university campuses within this city, the Christians numbered between ten and fifteen participants. One would be chosen to lead the worship, another would be chosen to teach. One would host the gathering and on selected meetings one would lead Communion. The interchanging leadership fostered variety within the worship services.

The important image to catch in this story is this small group of believers gathered in the middle of a large city, without support from the local church. Alone, they shared their faith in common, giving each other support, while struggling with their differences. Denomination meant little. It was the common faith that drew them together, a point of light surrounded by the forces of darkness. They huddled together in icy apartments, on uncomfortable chairs, for a bit of comfort in their faith.

In the western world, we have an abundance of churches. If you don't like the flavor of your assembly, simply go down the street to the next congregation and give that a whirl. The concept of one church, one group of believers, one choice is very alien to American Christians.

Lynn struggled to set aside her doubts about her fellow Christians when they met. She strove to concentrate on their common faith in Jesus Christ. These were her sisters and brothers, full of flaws, yet committed, just as she was, to sharing Jesus. They might have different styles, different approaches in how they treated others, how they spent their free time, their levels of maturity and spiritual growth. But the fact remained, that each had set aside their own comfort, their plans for the future, to spend this time in China.

On the Sundays that they shared Communion, a member of the group baked dense round loaves, each about five inches in diameter. The leader would break the bread in two before passing the platter around the group. Each would take a portion, chewing thoughtfully as they considered the broken body of Christ. A common cup came next, passed with a napkin for wiping the rim between sips. Those who might have a cold brought their own cups in order to keep from
infecting others. Some Sundays, Communion was set out and the members were encouraged to partake after a time of examining themselves. Other times, they would serve each other, saying, "This is Christ's body, broken for you."

During one such moment as Lynn took the bread into her mouth, the act of sharing Communion became a catalyst for all the grief she lived with in these alien conditions. The darkness closed in around her, the stress of her students, the grief over their sorrows, the confusion over her fellow teachers. All of it part of the darkness that had brought the son of God to earth in human form. This was why he had come, why he had taken up the challenge of redeeming man, of redeeming Lynn. In that moment, she understood that Jesus' sacrifice was for her. She was part of the crowd that condemned him, that drove him to the cross. No longer was it the dark hordes surrounding her. The dark forces were in her, compelling Jesus to offer up his life. She had been part of the darkness that surrounded him as he went to the cross, pressing in on all sides. She gagged on the bread. The desire to spit it out and fling herself from the room almost lifted her out of the chair.

"No, Jesus!" she cried silently. "Not this, not me. I didn't want to send you to the cross, your body broken for me."

In her thinking she had set herself apart from those living in darkness. This sacrifice was for those she served on a daily basis. She didn't want to be part of the darkness that required a blood sacrifice. Never had the struggle between God and Satan been so evident for her as in this dark city. And then she remembered the story of Peter. Think back to the first chapter.

Two men climbed the stone steps of a home in first century Jerusalem. They set wine, unleavened bread, a roast lamb on the table. The others in the room gathered to share their meal at Passover. But as they gathered, Jesus rose and tucked a towel into his belt. Kneeling before Peter, he lifted Peter's foot over a basin of water. In horror, Peter jerked his foot from Jesus' grasp.

"You will not wash my feet!" he cried hoarsely.

And Jesus replied quietly, "Unless I wash you, you will have no part of me."

One cannot doubt Peter's impulsive sincerity. When confronted by this choice, he responded with every ounce of submission.

"Then, Lord, not just my feet but my hands and my head as well!"

As Lynn recalled this account of the Passover with Jesus, she suddenly understood what was required of her. She must submit. Not just a part but all to the Lordship of Jesus Christ. That included her struggle with other Christians. That included the times when students impeded upon her privacy. That included her loneliness and culture shock. But most of all, she had to submit her right to make any choice at all. Jesus' sacrifice had been for all of this. 1

"This is my body, broken for you."

Her struggles were the nails and the splintered wood of her submission to God. She recalls that after Communion, as the group lifted their heads to face each other, it was as if the world was washed clean again for a few moments. The divisions between the members of that little body lifted. They talked, they cried, they celebrated their unity. On the following Monday, the divisions might creep back into place but for that moment they were free of all the grief that broke them into isolated centers of individuality. They were the body of Christ.

Lynn's experience in China is a microcosm of the church today. We see the church set in a dark world, the forces of evil arrayed against us. We are surrounded, our only hope in the one who gave his life for us. We need to understand this, to live this within the world-wide body of Christ. Rather than be torn apart by division or worse, by apathy, we must return to the renewal offered by the sacrament of Communion.

When we submit, confessing our wrongs against each other, the divisions begin to fall and we see what Christ intended for his people. We see what we will some day live in his presence. We share the joy of Christ. The covenant between God and man will be fully realized as we stand in God's presence.

After Word

I believe we are saved by faith in Jesus' death and resurrection alone. We are sanctified by his blood. His righteousness has been imputed to us through Jesus's death and resurrection. As we enter Communion, also called the Lord's Supper, we are commemorating a death. We are living a resurrection. Through that resurrection certain gifts and, in turn, responsibilities come to us. Once dead in our sins, we are now alive in Christ Jesus.

Commemoration and celebration are of the same fount. Like a fountain, God's grace flows from the Father, erupting in a great celebration of his gift of salvation to us. Under his blood, we have become the body of Christ. As individuals, we are the life blood pumping through every body of believers. The thoughts that stir us to action are the reality of Jesus Christ on earth, his living body as he sits on the right hand of God the Father.

As we accept that tiny wafer on our tongue, we are reminded that we are one in the Spirit with Christ. We are committed to allowing him to show himself through the action of our hands and feet, the words we speak, the choices we make about how we think. That is a weighty responsibility. Think about that the next time you allow the wafer and the wine to slide across your tongue.

Once again, another Sunday has arrived. The same encased glass and metal light fixtures dangle from the ceiling. The number of beams supporting the roof has not changed. I find myself back in a familiar seat, in the auditorium of the church that I have attended for the last thirty years. I'm wondering if I'm moldering in my seat. This thought horrifies me. Am I already so ossified that I cannot seek the vibrance of a living faith.

Once again, the Communion plate passes hand to hand down the row and we are called to examine ourselves. I have a choice. I can rip myself out of complacency and begin to examine the relationships of my life in light of the covenant with a God who is the same yesterday, today, forever. Or I can take the route of least resistance. Pass the plate, mutter a brief prayer for forgiveness for any sin I may have failed to confess in the last two weeks and swallow.

If we seek a vibrant relationship, founded in faith, with a living God, we must consider Communion as more than tradition. We must make it part of our practice of faith. We must challenge our complacency in our relationship with God and in turn, with others. After all, we have signed our names to a covenant written in his blood.

> *"He remembers his covenant forever,*
> *the word he commanded,*
> *for a thousand generations,*
> *the covenant he made with Abraham . . "*
> Psalms 105:8-9

AFTER WORD

"The time is coming, declares the Lord,
when I will make a new covenant
with the house of Israel
and with the house of Judah.
It will not be like the covenant
I made with their forefathers when I took them
by the hand to lead them out of Egypt,
because they did not remain faithful to my covenant,
and I turned away from them, declares the Lord.

This is the covenant I will make with the house of Israel
after that time, declares the Lord.
I will put my laws in their minds
and I will write them on their hearts.
I will be their God,
and they will be my people.
No longer will a man teach his neighbor,
or a man his brother,
saying, Know the Lord,
because they will all know me
from the least of them to the greatest.
For I will forgive their wickedness
and I will remember their sins no more.

Hebrews 8:8b-12

For many writers, finishing a book comes with mixed emotions. This book, for me, is really loaded. I am aware that I am a sinner saved by God's grace. I have not reached the perfection that God seeks in my life nor will I reach that point until I stand in God's presence. I'm looking forward to that day when struggle will cease and I will only marvel at my wonderful savior.

I will never feel as if I have finished this manuscript because I continue to grow in my faith. For those who have helped me grow, please accept a quiet thank you! For those who reviewed this manuscript: Martha, Christian, Don, Ken, Cath, Bill, Grace - each of you have give me a great gift of time and response to what I have written. Thank you many times over - you help me to be a better writer.

And finally to Darlene and Mike. Darlene, your quiet assurance that you would read what I wrote when I was 12 years old has stayed with me despite the jeers of our dorm mates. Thank you for granting me the thought that I might have something to say worth your time. What a gift! And Mike, even as we went our separate ways, you expressed a belief that God would use my gift some day to his honor and glory. I believe that this book is reaching for that goal. Let's us both keep reaching!

To him who sits on the throne, all glory and honor, forever!

Notes

In common:
1. Webster's New World Dictionary, c. 1991

Chapter 1:
1. Matthew 26:24-26
2. Matthew 26:29
3. Luke 5:17-26
4. Hebrews 9:22

Chapter 2:
1. *Covenant Marriage in Comparative Perspective*, John Witte Jr. & Eliza Ellison, www.eerdmans.com, 2005
2. Mark 15:38
3. Hebrews 9:15
4. *The Twilight Labyrinth*, George Otis Jr.; published by Chosen Books, a division of Baker Book House Co.; copyright1997; pg. 136.
5. Ibid, pg. 142
6. Ibid, pg. 144-145

Chapter 4:
1. Hebrews 10:25
2. I Corinthians 11:27
3. *Forgiving the Unforgivable*, Dr. David Stoops, published by Revell 2001
4. *A Long Obedience in the Same Direction*, Eugene H. Peterson, published by InterVarsity Press 1980, pg. 173

Chapter 5
1. The Passover included four cups of wine, each commemorating God's deliverance of Israel. Briefly, the first cup celebrated the sanctification both the Jews and we, in turn, have received as God's chosen ones. The second cup reminded the Jews that God brought them out of the slavery

as they could not effect their own release. It reminds us that we were also slaves to sin and God bought us with his blood. The third cup, also of deliverance, remembers the price that was paid for our redemption. The fourth cup was one of hope as the Jews look forward to Elijah as a guest and we look to Jesus, our redeemer. Jesus did not drink this last cup with his disciples but promised to drink with them after he returned from God the Father to reclaim his people.
2. I Peter 4:8

Chapter 6
1. *Leap Over A Wall*, Eugene Peterson, published by Harper Collins 1997
2. I Samuel 27 - 30

Chapter 9
1. John 13:2-9

www.ingramcontent.com/pod-product-compliance
Lightning Source LLC
Chambersburg PA
CBHW070627300426
44113CB00010B/1692